# Lifesaver Lessons
# MATH
## GRADE 4

## What Are Lifesaver Lessons?

### What Are Lifesaver Lessons?
Lifesaver Lessons™ are well-planned, easy-to-implement, curriculum-based lessons. Each lesson contains a complete materials list, step-by-step instructions, a reproducible activity or pattern, and several extension activities.

### How Do I Use A Lifesaver Lesson?
Each Lifesaver Lesson™ is designed to decrease your preparation time and increase the amount of quality teaching time with your students. These lessons are great for introducing or reinforcing new concepts. You may want to look through the lessons to see what types of materials to gather. After completing a lesson, be sure to check out the fun-filled extension activities.

### What Materials Will I Need?
Most of the materials for each lesson can be easily found in your classroom or school. Check the list of materials below for any items you may need to gather or purchase.

- crayons or colored pencils
- markers
- scissors
- glue
- tape
- chart paper
- centimeter rulers
- construction paper
- overhead projector
- blank transparencies
- transparency markers
- dice
- geoboards
- rubber bands
- small mirror
- dried beans
- colored chalk
- paper bag
- clock or watch with a second hand
- jelly beans

**Project Editor:**
Peggy W. Hambright

**Editors:**
Irving P. Crump, Debra Liverman

**Writers:**
Therese Durhman, Julie Eick Granchelli, Peggy W. Hambright, Elizabeth H. Lindsay, Debra Liverman, Gail Peckumn, Bonnie Pettifor, Barbara Samuels, Stephanie Willett-Smith

**Artists:**
Jennifer Tipton Bennett, Cathy Spangler Bruce, Clevell Harris, Mary Lester, Rob Mayworth, Barry Slate, Donna K. Teal

**Cover Artist:**
Jennifer Tipton Bennett

# Table Of Contents

**Manufactured in the United States**
10 9 8 7 6 5 4 3 2 1 0

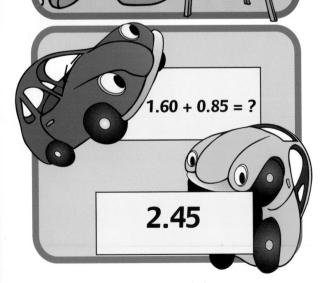

# On A Roll With Place Value

*Your students will be "die-ing" to take part in this fun place-value lesson.*

**Skills:** Recognizing place value; estimating totals

**Estimated Lesson Time:** 45 minutes

**Teacher Preparation:**
Make a copy of page 5 for each student.

**Materials:**
1 die for each pair of students
1 copy of page 5 for each student

| Hundreds | Tens | Ones |
|---|---|---|
| | | |
| | | |

**Background Information:**
Understanding place value is essential if students are to learn to add, subtract, multiply, and divide in a meaningful way. Place value allows any number to be represented using just ten digits (0–9). For example, the *2* in the number 342 has a different value than the *2* in the number 243, yet both are represented by the same digit.

## Introducing The Lesson:

Write 100,000; 10,000; 1,000; 100; 10; and 1 on the chalkboard. Then ask, "If you could receive one of these amounts as a weekly allowance, which one would you pick?" and "Which number would you select as the number of homework assignments you will have tonight?" After each question, have your students share the reasons they chose a particular amount over another.

## Steps:

1. Discuss place value and its effect on a numeral's value (see page 3).

2. Pair your students; then give each student a copy of page 5 and each pair one die. Instruct the partners to take turns rolling the die and recording the rolled number in either the ones, tens, hundreds, thousands, or ten thousands column of the place-value chart for that round. For example, if a player rolls a four, she can enter it in the ones column as *4,* the hundreds column as *400,* the ten thousands column as *40,000,* and so on.

3. Explain that when a player records her number in the tens column, she must write a zero in the ones column. Explain further that when she enters her number in the hundreds column, she must write one zero in the tens column and one zero in the ones column.

4. Point out that the object of the game is to be the player who gets closest to 100,000 without going over this amount in each round. Tell students that a round consists of ten die rolls—five rolls per player.

5. Direct the pairs to find the sum of their numbers after each round and determine which player's total is closer to 100,000 without going over. Instruct the pairs to award a point to the winner of each round.

6. Inform the students that if there is a tie, both players will receive a point and that if both players go over 100,000, neither player gets a point. Explain that the player with the most points at the end of eight rounds wins. Afterward have volunteers share the different strategies they used as the rounds progressed.

I won!

Congratulations!

Name_____ **Game Sheet**

Rounds Won By Me: _____
Rounds Won By My Partner: _____

### Round One

| | HTh | TTh | Th | H | T | O |
|---|---|---|---|---|---|---|
| Roll 1 | | | | | | |
| Roll 2 | | | | | | |
| Roll 3 | | | | | | |
| Roll 4 | | | | | | |
| Roll 5 | | | | | | |
| Sum | | | | | | |

### Round Two

| | HTh | TTh | Th | H | T | O |
|---|---|---|---|---|---|---|
| Roll 1 | | | | | | |
| Roll 2 | | | | | | |
| Roll 3 | | | | | | |
| Roll 4 | | | | | | |
| Roll 5 | | | | | | |
| Sum | | | | | | |

### Round Three

| | HTh | TTh | Th | H | T | O |
|---|---|---|---|---|---|---|
| Roll 1 | | | | | | |
| Roll 2 | | | | | | |
| Roll 3 | | | | | | |
| Roll 4 | | | | | | |
| Roll 5 | | | | | | |
| Sum | | | | | | |

### Round Four

| | HTh | TTh | Th | H | T | O |
|---|---|---|---|---|---|---|
| Roll 1 | | | | | | |
| Roll 2 | | | | | | |
| Roll 3 | | | | | | |
| Roll 4 | | | | | | |
| Roll 5 | | | | | | |
| Sum | | | | | | |

### Round Five

| | HTh | TTh | Th | H | T | O |
|---|---|---|---|---|---|---|
| Roll 1 | | | | | | |
| Roll 2 | | | | | | |
| Roll 3 | | | | | | |
| Roll 4 | | | | | | |
| Roll 5 | | | | | | |
| Sum | | | | | | |

### Round Six

| | HTh | TTh | Th | H | T | O |
|---|---|---|---|---|---|---|
| Roll 1 | | | | | | |
| Roll 2 | | | | | | |
| Roll 3 | | | | | | |
| Roll 4 | | | | | | |
| Roll 5 | | | | | | |
| Sum | | | | | | |

### Round Seven

| | HTh | TTh | Th | H | T | O |
|---|---|---|---|---|---|---|
| Roll 1 | | | | | | |
| Roll 2 | | | | | | |
| Roll 3 | | | | | | |
| Roll 4 | | | | | | |
| Roll 5 | | | | | | |
| Sum | | | | | | |

### Round Eight

| | HTh | TTh | Th | H | T | O |
|---|---|---|---|---|---|---|
| Roll 1 | | | | | | |
| Roll 2 | | | | | | |
| Roll 3 | | | | | | |
| Roll 4 | | | | | | |
| Roll 5 | | | | | | |
| Sum | | | | | | |

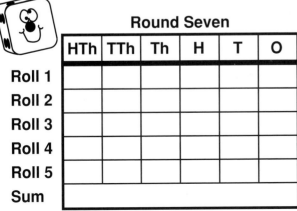
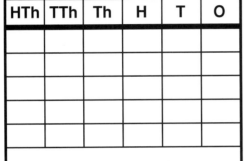
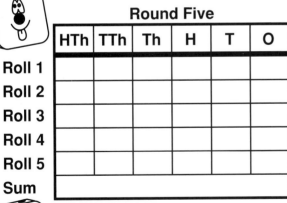

**Note To The Teacher:** Use with "Introducing The Lesson" on page 4.

## How To Extend The Lesson:

- Remove all tens and face cards from a standard deck of playing cards. Have each student draw a place-value chart and label its columns for thousands, hundreds, tens, and ones. To begin play, draw a card from the deck and read the numeral it contains aloud. Instruct your students to strategically place each announced numeral in one of the chart's columns in an effort to produce the largest number possible. Draw a total of four cards. Remind your students that once a numeral is recorded, it cannot be moved to another position on the chart. After determining which student built the largest number, repeat this procedure to play another round.

- Divide your class into groups of four. Give each group fourteen 4" x 6" index cards. Have each group cut its index cards in half to create twenty-eight 4" x 3" cards. Direct each group to create a set of place-value cards by writing *ones* on one card, *tens* on another card, and so on with *hundreds, thousands, ten thousands,* and *hundred thousands*. Next have each group create a set of number cards by writing a different six-digit number on each of the remaining index cards. Then instruct each group of four to subdivide into two pairs and place these two sets of cards facedown on a desk. Have one pair begin play by drawing a card from each stack. Direct this pair to identify the digit on its number card that has the place value written on its place-value card. Give each pair a point for every correct response it makes. Have the pairs take turns drawing cards in this manner until all of the number cards have been drawn. Declare the pair with the most points within each group the winner.

- Provide each student with highlighters of different colors and a page of car advertisements from your local newspaper. Challenge each student to color-code the digits in the price of each automobile according to their place value. For example, direct your students to color the ones-place digits yellow, the tens-place digits pink, the hundreds-place digits green, and so on. Afterward have volunteers share some of their color-coded numbers.

AUTO SALES

1992 Luxury Car....$5,995
All Power, Loaded!!!!!!!

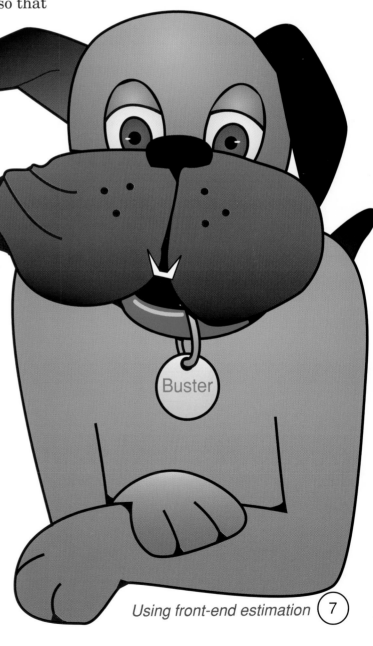

# Taking A Bite Out Of Estimation

*Chew on this deliciously good lesson about front-end estimation!*

**Skill:** Using front-end estimation

**Estimated Lesson Time:** 45 minutes

### Teacher Preparation:

1. Duplicate one copy of page 9 for each student.
2. Write any three-digit number on your overhead; then cover this number with a strip of paper so that its digits are not visible.

### Materials:

overhead projector
a strip of paper large enough
 to cover a three-digit number
1 copy of page 9 for each student

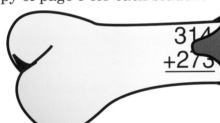

### Background Information:

*Front-end estimation* is a strategy that involves making two important observations about a given number: identifying its first—or front-end digit—and determining its place value. For example, in the problem above, the *3* and the *2* are the first digits in each addend, and both digits are in the hundreds place. To find this problem's sum by using front-end estimation, add 300 and 200 together to get 500.

## Introducing The Lesson:

Play a guessing game with your students. Explain that you want them to guess a number, but that you will provide them with only one of this number's three digits as a clue—the digit in the hundreds, the tens, or the ones place. Next have your class vote to determine which place value they want you to reveal. Afterward reveal the digit they wish to know. Next have each student write down a guess about what he thinks the number is; then uncover the number on your overhead. In turn, compare the number that was hidden with the one guessed by each of your students to see who made the closest guess.

## Steps:

1. Use different numbers to repeat the procedure above several more times.

2. With each number, ask your students which digit provides the most useful information for guessing what the number is. Point out that knowing the place value of the front-end digit is more useful than knowing the place value of the digit in the ones place, tens place, etc.

3. Next demonstrate how front-end estimation can be used with addition problems. Write the problem 345 + 567 vertically on your overhead. Point out that the front-end digits—the 3 in 345 and the 5 in 567—are both in the hundreds place. Cover all of the digits except for the 3 and 5. Ask your students to estimate the sum, knowing that the place value of the 3 and 5 is in the hundreds place. Help your students conclude that the estimated sum of this problem using front-end estimation is 800.

4. Write a different addition problem on your overhead. This time do not cover any digits. Ask your students to use front-end estimation to find the estimated sum for this problem. Remind them that they need to look only at the front-end digit of each numeral to make this estimate.

5. Give each student a copy of page 9 and have him follow the directions for additional practice with this strategy.

These are the front-end digits.

345
+567
800

Name_____

# Taking A Bite Out Of Estimation

Mr. Reitz gave Cory problems on flash cards to complete for homework. When he got home, Cory put the flash cards on the coffee table while he got a snack. Meanwhile, his dog chewed on the cards. Later Cory noticed his flash cards were missing big chunks of information. His mother suggested that he just estimate the answers. Help Cory solve his homework problems by using front-end estimation.

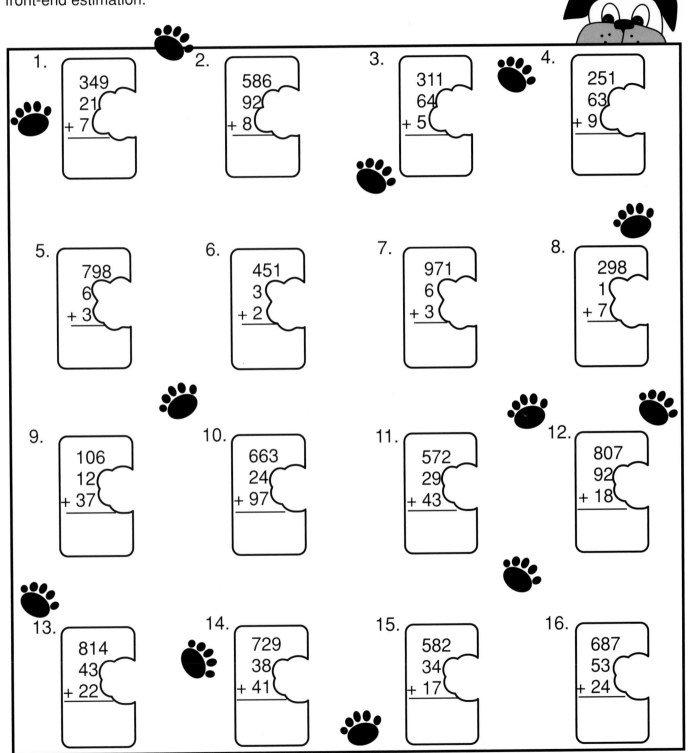

1.
```
  349
   21
+   7
_____
```

2.
```
  586
   92
+   8
_____
```

3.
```
  311
   64
+   5
_____
```

4.
```
  251
   63
+   9
_____
```

5.
```
  798
    6
+   3
_____
```

6.
```
  451
    3
+   2
_____
```

7.
```
  971
    6
+   3
_____
```

8.
```
  298
    1
+   7
_____
```

9.
```
  106
   12
+  37
_____
```

10.
```
  663
   24
+  97
_____
```

11.
```
  572
   29
+  43
_____
```

12.
```
  807
   92
+  18
_____
```

13.
```
  814
   43
+  22
_____
```

14.
```
  729
   38
+  41
_____
```

15.
```
  582
   34
+  17
_____
```

16.
```
  687
   53
+  24
_____
```

**Bonus Box:** On the back of this sheet, write four problems similar to the ones above. Challenge a classmate to solve your problems using front-end estimation.

⑨

## How To Extend The Lesson:

- Pair your students; then give each pair a grocery-store circular. Instruct each pair to use its circular to plan a dinner for ten people that costs less than $100. Remind the pairs to use front-end estimation to determine the estimated cost of this meal.

- Give your students several problems to work using the strategy of front-end estimation. Then have each student use a calculator to determine the closeness of his estimated answer to the actual answer.

- Collect several menus from a variety of restaurants in your area. For each menu, create a set of accompanying multiplication and division problems that require answers of estimated products or quotients. For example, "What is your estimate of the cost of ordering seven large pepperoni pizzas from Mama Mia's Pizzeria?" or "If three students split two orders of beef and broccoli from Fortune Garden, what would the approximate cost per person be?" Write each set of problems on a different card with art that suggests that restaurant. Store each menu and accompanying problems in a different envelope at a center for your students to use in their free time.

# May I Have Your Order, Please!

*Serve up a tall order on learning how to compare numbers!*

**Skill:** Comparing and ordering numbers to the hundred-thousands place

**Estimated Lesson Time:** 45 minutes

## Teacher Preparation:
1. Write the steps and examples for comparing and ordering numbers shown below on a sheet of chart paper.
2. Duplicate one copy of page 13 for each student.

## Materials:
1 sheet of chart paper
1 marker
1 sheet of paper and 1 pencil for each pair of students
1 copy of page 13 for each student

### To Compare Numbers:
**Step 1:** If one number has more digits than another, it is the greater number. If not, line up the digits in a column starting with the ones place. Begin at the left and compare to find the first place where the digits are different.

    **Example:** 12,630
                11,475
        same  different

**Step 2:** Compare the digits.
    **Example:** 2 > 1; so **12**,630 > **11**,475

### To Order Numbers:
**Step 1:** Same as Step 1 above.
    **Example:** 122,067
             12,251
             12,534
      same same  different

122,067 has more digits, so it is the greatest number.

**Step 2:** Same as Step 2 above.
    **Example:** 5 > 2; so 12,**5**34 > 12,**2**51

**Step 3:** Arrange the numbers in least to greatest order.
    **Example:** 12,251 < 12,534 < 122,067

## Background Information:
Numbers can be compared by lining up their digits by place value and looking for differences. To order a group of numbers, first compare their digits beginning with the greatest place value; then arrange the numbers in either a least-to-greatest or greatest-to-least order.

## Introducing The Lesson:

Show the class four similar objects of various sizes—such as books, pencils, or notepads. Ask your students to compare the size of these objects and arrange them in order from smallest to largest. Explain that comparing and ordering such objects sometimes involves examining one of their features, such as the length or width of one object compared with that of another. Further explain that in math, numbers can be compared and ordered in a similar manner.

## Steps:

1. Use the chart you programmed with the steps and examples on page 11 to explain how to compare and order numbers.

2. Pair your students. Next write the numerals *2, 3, 7, 1,* and *5* on the chalkboard. Instruct each pair to use those five digits to create the least *(12,357)* and greatest *(75,321)* numbers possible on loose-leaf paper. Then write "_____ < _____" on the chalkboard. Direct each pair to copy this inequality sentence and fill its blanks with the numbers just created *(12,357< 75,321)*. Ask a student volunteer to explain how she arrived at her answer. (*The 1 in the ten-thousands place is less than the 7 in the ten-thousands place, so 12,357 is less than 75,321.*)

3. Next direct each pair to use the same five digits to write a different five-digit number on paper and pass it to another pair. Instruct each pair to compare its new number with the two numbers in Step 2 above, and arrange all three numbers in an inequality sentence from least to greatest. In turn, have a volunteer from each pair record its inequality sentence on the chalkboard. After each inequality sentence has been recorded, direct your students to check it for accuracy. If any sentence is written incorrectly, challenge your students to correct it.

4. Give each student a copy of page 13. Instruct each student to follow the directions on the reproducible to complete the activity. Afterward have students discuss the answers together as a class.

Name_____

*Comparing and ordering numbers*

# Ordering Up Some Fascinating Facts!

Gerard Giraffe has gathered some fascinating facts about some of the tallest, longest, and largest man-made and geographic features in the world! But he needs a little help in comparing and ordering the facts. Follow the directions for each section below. Write each answer on the line provided.

1. Compare these numbers. How are they all alike?

   192,860        5,840        872        1,880

   _____

2. Compare the heights of the buildings below; then write an inequality sentence that lists their heights in order from least to greatest.

   Sears Tower 1,454 ft.          Nations Bank Tower 1,050 ft.
   Empire State Building 1,250 ft.   Chrysler Building 1,046 ft.
   World Trade Center 1,368 ft.    Amoco 1,136 ft.

   _____

3. Read the square miles of each lake listed below. Then complete each inequality sentence by filling in each blank with a different number. (Hint: There are several possible answer choices!)

   Caspian Sea 143,244      Superior 31,700
   Michigan 22,300          Malawi 11,150          Victoria 26,828

   _____ > _____          _____ < _____

4. Write the heights of these mountains in order from greatest to least.

   Kilimanjaro 19,340 ft.    Vinson Massif 16,864 ft.
   Everest 29,028 ft.        McKinley 20,320 ft.        Jaya 16,500 ft.

   _____

5. These are some of the world's most active volcanoes. Write them in order from least to greatest in height.

   Cameroun 13,350 ft.    Mauna Loa 13,680 ft.
   Acatenango 13,000 ft.  Galeras 13,400 ft.

   _____

6. Compare the square miles of each island. Which island is the greatest in square miles? Which is the least in square miles?

   New Guinea 317,000      Victoria Island 83,896
   Borneo 280,100          Sumatra 182,860
   Greenland 840,000       Great Britain 84,200

Now exchange papers with a friend and check each other's work.

**Bonus Box:** Choose any ten of the numbers listed above. On the back of this sheet, arrange the numbers in order from least to greatest.

(13)

©1997 The Education Center, Inc. • *Lifesaver Lessons* • Grade 4 • TEC506 • Key p. 95

## How To Extend The Lesson:

- Before beginning the activity, gather one index card per student and write a random number between 10 and 100,000 on each card. Shuffle the cards. Have each student choose one card. Then direct your students to form a line around the room and hold their cards facing outward so that the numbers can be seen. Instruct the student with the least number and the student with the greatest number to identify themselves. Direct these students to stand at the beginning and the end of the line, respectively. Finally, have each student position himself in order between these two students, beginning with the least number and ending with the greatest number.

- Use an opaque or overhead projector to create a large outline of your state. Then divide your students into groups of three. Assign each group a different topic to research about your state—such as population of major cities, square miles of major cities, number of employed workers, lengths of rivers, heights of mountains, and numbers of different species of plants or animals. Direct each group to research its topic for five numerical facts, placing the facts in order from least to greatest. Next instruct each group to draw a colorful picture symbolizing its topic on the state outline, recording the ordered facts next to that symbol. Finally have each group share its facts; then display the outline on a large wall or bulletin board titled "[State Name], A State Made To Order!"

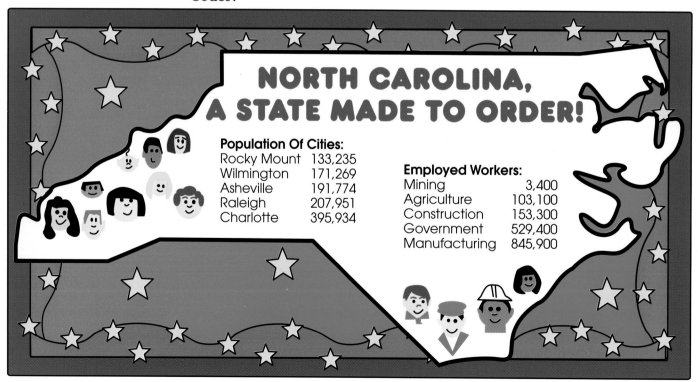

### NORTH CAROLINA, A STATE MADE TO ORDER!

**Population Of Cities:**

| | |
|---|---|
| Rocky Mount | 133,235 |
| Wilmington | 171,269 |
| Asheville | 191,774 |
| Raleigh | 207,951 |
| Charlotte | 395,934 |

**Employed Workers:**

| | |
|---|---|
| Mining | 3,400 |
| Agriculture | 103,100 |
| Construction | 153,300 |
| Government | 529,400 |
| Manufacturing | 845,900 |

# Tinkering With Tangrams

*Enhance the meaning of geometric terms by exploring tangrams.*

**Skill:** Identifying, describing, comparing, and classifying geometric figures

**Estimated Lesson Time:** 1 hour

**Teacher Preparation:**
1. Duplicate one copy of the top portion of page 17 for each student on the thickest paper possible.
2. Make an overhead transparency of the bottom portion of page 17.

**Materials:**
1 copy of the tangrams pattern at the top of page 17 for each student
1 sheet of chart paper for each group of students
1 blank transparency for creating a transparency of the bottom portion of page 17
scissors

**Background Information:**
A *polygon* is a two-dimensional shape, formed from three or more line segments that lie within one plane. A *regular* polygon has sides of equal length and angles of equal size. An *irregular* polygon has unequal sides and unequal angles. Polygons that are exactly the same size and shape are *congruent,* and those that are the same shape but not identical in size are *similar.*

- *Triangles* are polygons that have three sides and three angles.
- *Quadrilaterals* are polygons that have four sides and four angles.
- *Parallelograms* are quadrilaterals that have parallel line segments in both pairs of opposite sides.
- *Trapezoids* are quadrilaterals that have a pair of parallel sides.
- *Rectangles* are parallelograms with four right angles.
- *Squares* are rectangles that have sides of equal length.
- *Pentagons* are polygons that have five sides and five angles.
- *Hexagons* are polygons that have six sides and six angles.

*Exploring geometric figures* 15

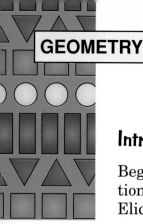

## Introducing The Lesson:

Begin this lesson by displaying the transparency that you created of the bottom portion of page 17. Review the names of these six geometric shapes with your students. Elicit brief descriptions of these shapes—number of sides, types of angles, etc.—from your students (see page 15).

## Steps:

1. Divide your class into six groups; then give each group a sheet of chart paper. Give one copy of the tangrams pattern on the top of page 17 to each student. Instruct her to cut out each of the seven tangram pieces.

2. Borrow a set of cutouts and chart paper from one of your groups; then demonstrate how to trace the shape of a hexagon onto chart paper so that each tangram piece used in that shape is recognizable (see the illustration). Also demonstrate how to label the shape as hexagon ABCDEF.

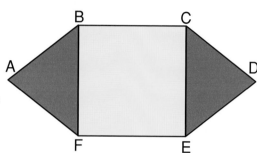

3. Assign each group one of the shapes from the transparency—square, rectangle, parallelogram, trapezoid, pentagon, or triangle.

4. Explain that each group member will have 20 minutes to create and label her assigned shape in as many different ways as she can. Establish that the shapes she creates can be regular or irregular and—depending on her assigned shape—can be formed from any combination of two or more, even all seven of her tangram pieces. Point out, too, that she can trace the same piece more than once if she wishes.

5. When time is up, direct the members of each group to take turns naming the tangram pieces used in each of their tracings (see the answer key on page 95 for possible drawings).

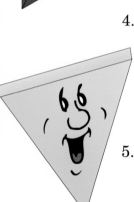

6. Afterward review geometric terms by discussing the questions below.
   - Which groups made polygons? *(every group)*
   - Which groups made quadrilaterals? *(the groups that were assigned the parallelogram, trapezoid, square, and rectangle)*
   - Which groups made parallelograms? *(the groups that were assigned the parallelogram, square, and rectangle)*
   - Which groups made rectangles? *(the groups that were assigned the rectangle and square)*
   - Name the congruent, similar, regular, and irregular drawings on your group's chart paper. *(Answers will vary.)*

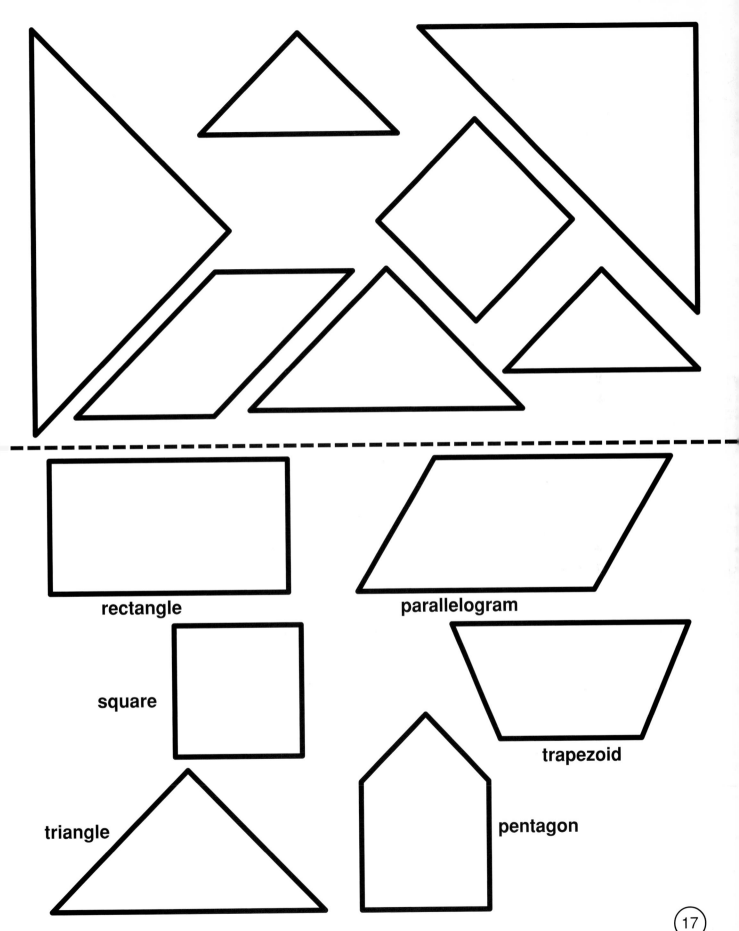

rectangle

parallelogram

square

trapezoid

triangle

pentagon

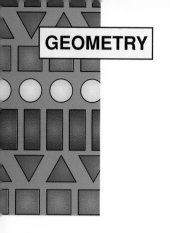

## How To Extend The Lesson:

- Have your students explore further with tangram pieces to create other shapes—such as a hexagon, a rhombus, or even an irregular nonagon. Direct your students to trace the shapes they create onto multicolored drawing paper. Next have the students cut out and glue each shape to another sheet of paper, labeling it according to the number of sides the new shape has (see the illustration on the left). Then display your students' cutouts on a bulletin board titled "Tangrams Taking Shape."

- Duplicate 8–10 copies of the tangram pieces at the top of page 17. Have a student volunteer cut out these pieces. Afterward place all of the tangram pieces inside a bag. Shake the bag; then randomly distribute two different cutouts to each student. Direct him to write five sentences that compare his two shapes on a large index card. Next instruct him to paste both of his shapes onto a sheet of construction paper and tape his index card to this paper's bottom edge (see the illustration on the right). Then display your students' papers on a bulletin board titled "Shapely Comparisons."

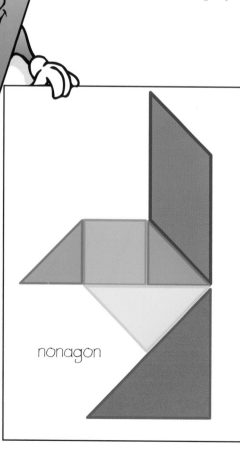

nonagon

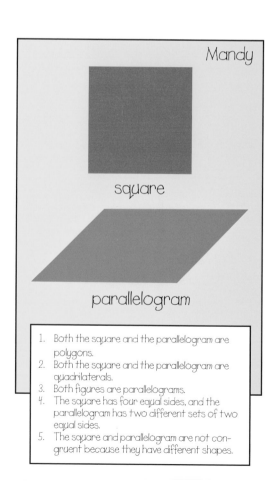

Mandy

square

parallelogram

1. Both the square and the parallelogram are polygons.
2. Both the square and the parallelogram are quadrilaterals.
3. Both figures are parallelograms.
4. The square has four equal sides, and the parallelogram has two different sets of two equal sides.
5. The square and parallelogram are not congruent because they have different shapes.

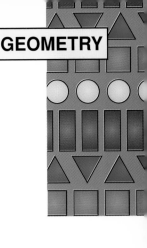

# Angling For Angles

*Cast out this exciting lesson on angles
and watch your students reel in some learning!*

**Skill:** Identifying and constructing acute, obtuse, and right angles

**Estimated Lesson Time:** 45 minutes

**Teacher Preparation:**
Duplicate one copy of page 21 for each student.

**Materials:**
1 copy of page 21 for each student
1 geoboard and geobands for each student or pair of students

**90°**

**90° – 180°**

**Background Information:**
    An *angle* is a figure formed by two rays that share the same endpoint. A *ray* is a part of a line that extends in one direction from a point. The common endpoint of two rays forming an angle is called the *vertex*.
    An angle's size is usually measured in degrees. *Right angles* are formed when the two rays make a square corner, measuring exactly 90 degrees. *Acute angles* measure less than 90 degrees, and *obtuse angles* measure between 90 and 180 degrees.

 **less than 90°**

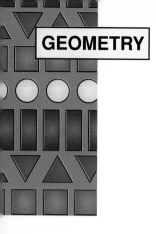
## Introducing The Lesson:

Ask a student volunteer to draw two rays on the board. Then have a different student volunteer draw two rays that share a common endpoint. Explain that this common endpoint is called a vertex and that the two rays form an angle. Tell the class that they will be learning about three types of angles—right, acute, and obtuse.

## Steps:

**Step 1**

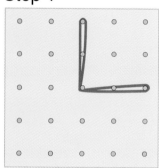

1. Review the definitions for the three types of angles on page 19. Give each student—or pair of students—a geoboard and geobands. Ask each student to use the geobands to form an angle resembling the corner of a rectangle on her geoboard. Explain that this angle is called a right angle.

2. Point out that the distance between two sides of an angle is measured in degrees. Tell your students that a right angle measures 90 degrees. Draw a right angle on the board, inserting the symbol for the right angle—a small square—in the vertex. Explain that a right angle is often pictured with this square symbol in its vertex.

**Step 4**

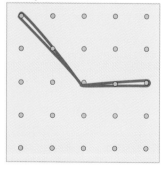

3. Direct each student to construct several more right angles on her geoboard.

4. Next remind each student that an acute angle measures less than 90 degrees. Then challenge each student to use what she knows about the measurement of a right angle and the measurement of an acute angle to construct an acute angle on her geoboard. Circulate around the room to check the angle built by each child, offering guidance to students who need clarification. Have each child form several more acute angles.

**Step 5**

5. Explain that an obtuse angle measures more than 90 degrees. Challenge each student to construct an obtuse angle on her geoboard. Again, circulate to check for accuracy; then have each child build several more obtuse angles on her geoboard.

6. Draw several angles of each type on the board, asking student volunteers to identify each angle by name.

7. Give each student a copy of page 21 for additional practice with angles.

Name _____

# Angling Around Town

Each time you turn a corner in your car, the car's path makes an invisible angle. Study the street map of the town of Angler below. Then read each set of directions below the map and write the type of angle— *acute, obtuse,* or *right*—that your car's path would form when making that turn.

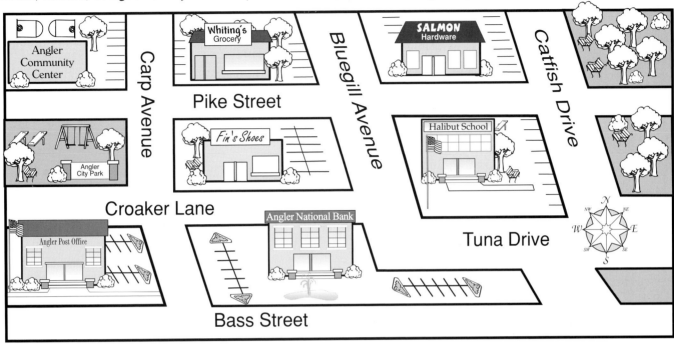

1. If you were heading east on Croaker Lane and turned southeast onto Carp Avenue, your car's path would be a(n) _____ angle.

2. If you were traveling west on Bass Street and then turned northeast onto Catfish Drive, your car's path would be a(n) _____ angle.

3. If you were heading east on Pike Street and turned north onto Carp Avenue, your car's path would be a(n) _____ angle.

4. If you were driving west on Tuna Drive and turned northwest onto Bluegill Avenue, your car's path would be a(n) _____ angle.

5. If you were heading southeast on Catfish Drive and turned west onto Pike Street, your car's path would be a(n) _____ angle.

6. If you were driving northwest on Bluegill Avenue and turned west onto Pike Street, your car's path would be a(n) _____ angle.

7. How would you get from the Angler National Bank to Salmon Hardware if your car could only make right-angled turns to get there? _____
   _____

8. How would you get from the Angler Post Office to Halibut School if your car could only make acute-angled turns? _____
   _____

**Bonus Box:** List the number and kinds of turns you would make if you traveled southeast down Catfish Drive, west on Tuna Drive, northwest on Bluegill Avenue, west on Croaker Lane, north on Carp Avenue, and west on Pike Street to reach Angler Community Center.

(21)

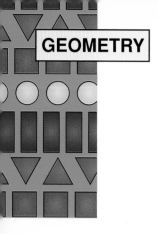

## How To Extend The Lesson:

- Explain to your students that figures made up of straight line segments all contain various combinations of acute, obtuse, and right angles. On the board or an overhead projector, draw some common shapes—such as a triangle, a pentagon, a hexagon, an octagon, a parallelogram, a trapezoid, a star, a Christmas tree, and a cross. Then have each student list the types of angles found in each shape.

- Make three columns on the board, heading the first column "Acute," the second column "Right," and the third column "Obtuse." Review the three types of angles; then have each student copy the columns onto loose-leaf paper. Together, look around the room to find one example of each type of angle to list under the appropriate column. For example, a single hole puncher could go under "Acute," loose-leaf paper under "Right," and the letter *Y* under "Obtuse." Then challenge each student to extend her list by adding three examples of acute angles, three examples of obtuse angles, and five examples of right angles. Afterward invite each child to share her list with the class. Each time a different item is named, record it under the appropriate column on the board.

- Include a review of time when you teach your lesson on angles. Give each student a small clock with movable hands. Call out different times of the day; then have each student move the hands of his clock to represent that time and identify the type of angle formed by the clock's hands. If movable clock faces are not available, duplicate a sheet of clock faces without hands so that each student can draw in the hands to show the type of angle that's formed.

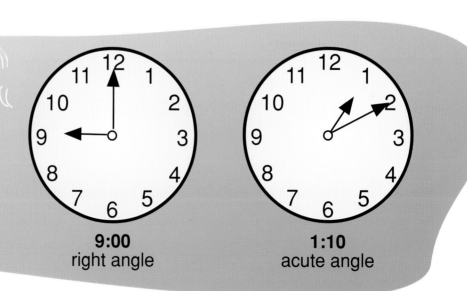

**9:00**
right angle

**1:10**
acute angle

# Sewing Up Symmetry

*Sharpen your students' skills in symmetry by getting right to the point!*

**Skill:** Recognizing and constructing symmetrical figures

**Estimated Lesson Time:** 45 minutes

## Teacher Preparation:
1. Duplicate one copy of page 25 for each student.
2. Use a permanent black marker to draw a solid line lengthwise down the center of a blank transparency.

## Materials:
1 copy of page 25 for each student
1 permanent black marker
1 blank transparency
overhead projector
overhead pattern blocks (or an overhead pen to draw shapes)
1 sheet of loose-leaf paper for each student
scissors
1 sheet of red 8" x 8" construction paper
1 handheld mirror

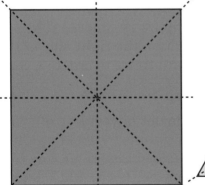

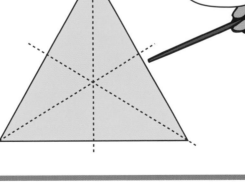

*The dashed lines running through each shape represent lines of symmetry.*

## Background Information:
A figure is *symmetrical* if a line divides it into two congruent or equal parts. The two parts are like mirror images of one another. Some figures have no lines of symmetry at all. Others may have anywhere from one to an infinite number of lines of symmetry.

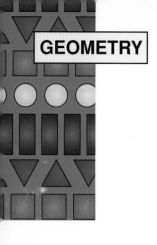

## Introducing The Lesson:

Explain to your students that you wish to make a heart cutout. Ask them how you might make an attractive heart using only a sheet of red construction paper and a pair of scissors. Guide your students to conclude that folding the paper in half before cutting it is one way to create the heart shape. Next fold the paper in half and cut out half of a heart shape, but do not open it up. Ask students if they know what the heart will look like. Hold the folded heart shape next to a mirror; then ask a student if the resulting image resembles what the opened paper will look like. Explain that by folding the paper in half and cutting out the shape, a symmetrical—or mirror—image has been formed.

## Steps:

1. Point out to your students that the fold in the heart shape is the figure's *line of symmetry*. Explain that a line of symmetry divides the figure into two congruent or equal parts.

2. On the overhead, display the transparency you created. Explain that just as the fold in the heart was the line of symmetry, the vertical line on the transparency will act as the line of symmetry for the next activity.

3. Place a triangular pattern block—or draw a triangle—on the left side of the line of symmetry. Show how a symmetrical figure can be made by placing an identical triangular shape on the right side of the line of symmetry.

4. Continue by placing a different shape on the left side of the line. Ask a student volunteer to make the figure symmetrical by selecting a matching shape and positioning it on the right side of the line of symmetry. Repeat this process several times to create a complex design.

5. Tell your students that some figures do not have a line of symmetry while others have one or more lines of symmetry. Hold up the heart cutout and ask students if it could be folded any other way to show perfect symmetry. Have a student volunteer try to fold the heart in different ways to find additional lines of symmetry.

6. Ask your students to take out a sheet of loose-leaf paper. Challenge each student to fold his paper to find as many lines of symmetry as possible. Invite each student to share his findings with the class.

7. Give each student a copy of page 25 for additional practice with symmetry.

# Stick With It

Grandma Porcupine is in a "sticky" situation and needs your help. She has started a quilt for her grandson's birthday and needs help getting it finished by next week. Grandma wants each quilt block to be perfectly symmetrical. Avoid getting "stuck" with a mistake on a quilt square by first shading each square in with a pencil. Once you are sure the design is symmetrical, color it with a marker.

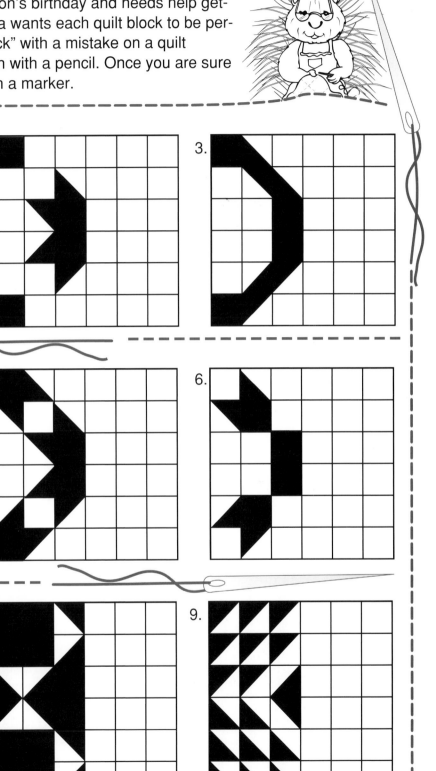

**Bonus Box:** On a sheet of graph paper, design some colorful quilt squares of your own.

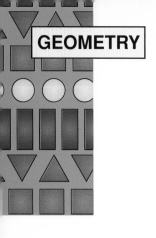

## How To Extend The Lesson:

- Provide each student with a rectangular sheet of white construction paper. Assign each student a specific country from the list below. Have the student find that country's flag in an encyclopedia and draw it on her sheet of paper. Direct the student to color the flag; then have her draw all of the flag's lines of symmetry. Display the flags on a bulletin board labeled "Flagging Down Symmetry."

| | | | |
|---|---|---|---|
| Trinidad and Tobago | Yemen | Ireland | Ethiopia |
| Armenia | Austria | Italy | Gambia |
| Kuwait | Belarus | Latvia | Ivory Coast |
| Laos | Belgium | Lithuania | Mali |
| Indonesia | Bulgaria | Luxembourg | Niger |
| Palau | Estonia | Monaco | Nigeria |
| Syria | Germany | Netherlands | South Africa |
| Tajikistan | France | Romania | Canada |
| Thailand | Hungary | Switzerland | Honduras |
| United Arab Emirates | Iceland | Vietnam | Jamaica |

- Challenge each student to search through old magazines and cut out pictures that show symmetry in rugs, bedspreads, furniture, appliances, and food. Instruct each student to use a marker and ruler to draw all the lines of symmetry on each item. Direct each student to share his collection of symmetrical items with the class; then have him contribute his items for gluing onto a large sheet of chart paper to make a classroom mural.

- Invite each student to bring some Lego® blocks to school. Pair your students, giving each partner her own pile of Legos®. Direct each child to construct a simple shape using the blocks. Have each child exchange her shape with her partner and try to build a symmetrical—or mirror—image of the shape she receives. Encourage each student to share her results with the rest of the class.

- Cut out one magazine photograph of a person's face for every two students in your classroom. Then cut each photo exactly down the middle lengthwise. Explain to your students that many people think the human face is symmetrical. Then ask students if they agree or disagree with this belief. Allow each child to look in a mirror and determine if his face is exactly symmetrical. Give each child half of a face and direct him to glue it to a sheet of construction paper. Challenge each student to draw the missing part of the face he received, making it as symmetrical as possible. Post the completed work on a bulletin board under the heading "The Beauty Of Symmetry."

# Pick A Peck Of Patterns

*Pepper your students' math practice with*
*opportunities to recognize and continue patterns.*

**Skill:** Recognizing and continuing established patterns

**Estimated Lesson Time:** 45 minutes

## Teacher Preparation:
1. Duplicate a copy of page 29 for each student.
2. Collect several items that have continuing patterns—fabric swatches, wallpaper samples, bulletin-board borders, etc.

## Materials:
1 copy of page 29 for each student
sample objects with
    patterns

## Background Information:
The ability to recognize and describe patterns helps students understand mathematical functions and relationships. Repeating patterns can be found in nature, in spoken and written words, in musical forms and video images, and in ornamental designs and structures. For example: red, white, red, white, red, white; square, circle, circle, square, circle, circle, square; 3, 3, 3, 4, 3, 3, 3, 4.

## Introducing The Lesson:

Begin this lesson by having eight students come to the front of the class. Have every other student kneel while the others stand. Ask the rest of the class to define the pattern that these students make. Afterward challenge your students to name several objects in the classroom that contain patterns.

## Steps:

1.  Display the objects with patterns that you collected earlier.

2.  Show each object one at a time to see if your students can determine and explain each pattern.

3.  Challenge each student to create a repeating pattern of his own on notebook paper. Suggest that he make a pattern that repeats shapes, colors, numbers, letters, or words. Then have the student substitute a blank answer line for one of the elements of his pattern.

4.  Next direct each student to exchange his paper with a classmate and supply the missing part of his classmate's pattern.

5.  Afterward have each student explain how he determined the missing part of the pattern.

6.  Give each student a copy of page 29 and have him follow its directions.

CHICKEN CHOW

# Pick A Peck Of Patterns

The chef at the local pizza parlor has a problem. The green peppers he needs to make a pizza are not in the usual spot in the refrigerator. Help him find these misplaced peppers by filling in the missing part of each pattern below.

Then use the secret code at the bottom of this sheet to find the letter that matches each answer. If you arrange these vowels and consonants correctly, you'll spell the location of the missing peppers. Good luck!

1. 2, 3, 4, 6, 6, 9, 8, 12, 10, 15, _____
   **Letter code:** _____

2. 48, 88, 24, 44, 12, _____, 6, 11, 3
   **Letter code:** _____

3. B, E, I, _____, T
   **Letter code:** _____

4. 10000001, _____, 100001, 10001, 1001, 101
   **Letter code:** _____

5. A, E, H, L, O, S, _____, Z
   **Letter code:** _____

6. 1, 2, 4, 8, _____, 32, 64, 128, 256
   **Letter code:** _____

7. N, Y, N, Y, Y, N, N, Y, N, _____, Y, N, Y
   **Letter code:** _____

8. 144, 89, 55, 34, _____, 13, 8, 5, 3, 2, 1, 1
   **Letter code:** _____

9. ■ ■ ▼ ■ ▲ ■ ■ ▼ _____ ▲ ■ ■ ▼ ■ ▲ ■ ■
   **Letter code:** _____

10. ▼ ▼ ▼ ▼ ▼ ▼ ■ ▼ ▼ ▼ ▼ _____ ▼ ▼ ▼ ▼ ■ ■ ▼ ▼ ▼ ■ ■ ■ ■
    **Letter code:** _____

11. 14, 9, 12, 7, _____, 5, 8, 3, 6, 1, 4
    **Letter code:** _____

| N | V | Y | 1000001 | 10 | 12 | 16 | 21 | 22 | ■ | ■■ |
|---|---|---|---------|----|----|----|----|----|----|----|
| E | R | P | C | T | P | A | P | H | E | P |

The missing peppers are in the

___ ___ ___ ___ ___ ___   ___ ___ ___ ___ ___!
 C   V   C   C   V   C     C   V   C   C   C

**Bonus Box:** Create several patterns of your own on the back of this sheet.

## How To Extend The Lesson:

- Have your students work in pairs to form as many different pentominos as they can with five same-sized squares. Remind your students that a pentomino consists of five squares, and that each square must share a full side with another square in the same figure. Direct the pairs to trace the pentominos that they create and share them with the class. If desired, place these sets of pentomino squares at a center along with a challenge to duplicate some of the patterns that were shared during free time.

- Give each student a wallpaper sample that contains a complex design. Direct the student to glue her sample to the center of a sheet of unlined paper. Then challenge her to continue this wallpaper pattern on her paper, extending the pattern in all directions.

- Have your students work together in groups of eight to create a people pattern based on human attributes. Suggest that each group form its pattern based upon just one characteristic—hair color, eye color, sex, or clothing style. For example, one group might line up according to the eye colors of its members: brown eyes, brown eyes, blue eyes, brown eyes, brown eyes, blue eyes, brown eyes, brown eyes. Then instruct each group in turn to act out its pattern for the class. As each group shares, challenge the remaining groups to identify the pattern and name the attribute being featured.

- Give each student a copy of a monthly calendar and have him select a date of the month that is surrounded on all sides by other dates. For example, a student could choose the date of the third Wednesday in August because it is surrounded on all sides by other dates. Next direct each student to find the sum of all the dates in the square that surrounds his selected date. Then help him discover that the sum of these dates (including the chosen date) is nine times the number that he selected. Share and explain the following grid for this pattern.

| | August | | | | | |
|---|---|---|---|---|---|---|
| **S** | **M** | **T** | **W** | **T** | **F** | **S** |
| | | | | | 1 | 2 |
| 3 | 4 | 5 | 6 | 7 | 8 | 9 |
| 10 | 11 | 12 | 13 | 14 | 15 | 16 |
| 17 | 18 | 19 | 20 | 21 | 22 | 23 |
| 24 | 25 | 26 | 27 | 28 | 29 | 30 |
| 31 | | | | | | |

$n$ = selected date

$n - 8 = 12$    $n - 7 = 13$    $n - 6 = 14$

$n - 1 = 19$    $n = 20$    $n + 1 = 21$

$n + 6 = 26$    $n + 7 = 27$    $n + 8 = 28$

# Patterns Aplenty

*Help your students see that patterns
are everywhere—even in multiplication and division problems!*

**Skill:** Observing multiplication and division patterns

**Estimated Lesson Time:** 45 minutes

## Teacher Preparation:
1. Duplicate one copy of page 33 for each student.
2. Gather pictures from magazines or books that illustrate patterns in the environment; then duplicate one copy of these pattern pictures for each pair of students.
3. Gather one hundreds board (or enlarge and duplicate the hundreds-board pattern on page 32). Also gather one handful of beans or other hundreds-board markers for each pair of students.

## Materials:
1 copy of page 33 for each student
1 hundreds board (or 1 enlarged and duplicated hundreds-board pattern from page 32) for each pair of students
1 handful of beans or other hundreds-board markers for each pair of students
1 copy of the duplicated pattern pictures for each pair of students

Check out my pattern!

## Background Information:
Pattern concepts are a central theme woven throughout all mathematics. Observing patterns in events, designs, shapes, pictures, and sets of numbers helps students see that patterns are the essence of math. Students who can identify patterns and express them in mathematical terms begin to see how math applies to the world in which they live.

## Introducing The Lesson:

Pair your students; then distribute one copy of each pattern picture that you duplicated earlier to each pair. Instruct the pair to find as many patterns in each picture as possible. Allow each pair to share one of the patterns it finds with the class. Explain that patterns can be found not only in the environment but in numbers as well.

## Steps:

1. Give each pair one hundreds board and a handful of beans or other hundreds-board markers. Explain that you will give directions for them to follow on their hundreds boards. Establish that if your directions are followed correctly, a visual pattern should appear on each hundreds board.

2. Instruct each pair to cover all the numbers whose digits add together to equal nine. For example, the digits in the number 18 total nine: 1 + 8 = 9. Ask each pair if the covered numbers have anything else in common. Help your students conclude that the covered numbers are all multiples of nine.

3. Direct each pair to clear its board. Next have each pair cover all the multiples of four, leading the pairs through the four times tables if necessary to help them identify all the multiples. Discuss the visual pattern created by covering these multiples.

4. Again have the pairs clear their hundreds boards; then instruct each pair to cover all the multiples of three. Demonstrate how to use skip counting to find all the multiples beyond the number 36. Have students observe the resulting visual pattern.

5. Give each pair 15 minutes to create any three additional patterns on its hundreds board, using multiples other than those already explored. Then instruct each pair to describe its new patterns and how they were discovered on a sheet of loose-leaf paper.

6. Give your students more practice in observing patterns in pictures by distributing one copy of page 33 to each student. Instruct him to complete the sheet as directed.

| 1 | 2 | 3 | 4 | 5 | 6 | 7 | 8 | 9 | 10 |
|---|---|---|---|---|---|---|---|---|-----|
| 11 | 12 | 13 | 14 | 15 | 16 | 17 | 18 | 19 | 20 |
| 21 | 22 | 23 | 24 | 25 | 26 | 27 | 28 | 29 | 30 |
| 31 | 32 | 33 | 34 | 35 | 36 | 37 | 38 | 39 | 40 |
| 41 | 42 | 43 | 44 | 45 | 46 | 47 | 48 | 49 | 50 |
| 51 | 52 | 53 | 54 | 55 | 56 | 57 | 58 | 59 | 60 |
| 61 | 62 | 63 | 64 | 65 | 66 | 67 | 68 | 69 | 70 |
| 71 | 72 | 73 | 74 | 75 | 76 | 77 | 78 | 79 | 80 |
| 81 | 82 | 83 | 84 | 85 | 86 | 87 | 88 | 89 | 90 |
| 91 | 92 | 93 | 94 | 95 | 96 | 97 | 98 | 99 | 100 |

# Picture-Perfect Patterns

Study the picture above. Then, for each object or group of objects listed below, write a number sentence to explain the pattern that can be found. Remember: There can be more than one way to write each pattern.

1. the flowers on top of the bookcase:

_____

2. the rug under the table:

_____

3. the books on the top shelf of the bookcase:

_____

4. the leaves on the floor plant:

_____

5. the plates on the table:

_____

6. the silverware on the table:

_____

7. Draw a different arrangement of books for each of the three empty bookshelves in the picture. Write a number sentence to explain each pattern that you create.

Shelf 2: _____

Shelf 3: _____

Shelf 4: _____

**Bonus Box:** Without getting out of your chair, find three patterns within your classroom. On the back of this sheet, write a number sentence and an explanation for each pattern you find.

## How To Extend The Lesson:

• Emphasize patterns in multiplication and division by showing students a shortcut when multiplying or dividing multiples of ten. Write the two sets of equations shown below on the chalkboard. Have students look for a pattern in each set of equations. Then explain how to use patterns with the zeros to make multiplying and dividing multiples of ten easier *(count the zeros)*.

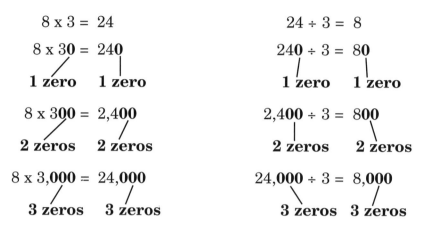

$$8 \times 3 = 24 \qquad\qquad 24 \div 3 = 8$$
$$8 \times 30 = 240 \qquad\qquad 240 \div 3 = 80$$
$$\text{1 zero} \quad \text{1 zero} \qquad\qquad \text{1 zero} \quad \text{1 zero}$$
$$8 \times 300 = 2{,}400 \qquad\qquad 2{,}400 \div 3 = 800$$
$$\text{2 zeros} \quad \text{2 zeros} \qquad\qquad \text{2 zeros} \quad \text{2 zeros}$$
$$8 \times 3{,}000 = 24{,}000 \qquad\qquad 24{,}000 \div 3 = 8{,}000$$
$$\text{3 zeros} \quad \text{3 zeros} \qquad\qquad \text{3 zeros} \quad \text{3 zeros}$$

• Duplicate 11 copies of a 12 x 12 multiplication table for each group of students. Divide your class into groups of three or four students. Instruct each group to color a different table for the multiples of each of the following numbers: 2, 3, 4, 5, 6, 7, 8, 9, 10, 11, and 12 (see the examples below). Have each group color the boxes of the multiples in each table, using a different color for each table. Allow your students to use calculators to help with the multiplication as needed. After the tables have been colored, discuss which tables have the same patterns or similar characteristics. Finally challenge your students to predict the resulting visual patterns created by coloring multiples of numbers greater than 12, such as 13 or 15.

> Every number shaded on the 6 times table is also shaded on the 3 times table!

| 1 | 2 | 3 | 4 | 5 | 6 | 7 | 8 | 9 | 10 | 11 | 12 |
|---|---|---|---|---|---|---|---|---|---|---|---|
| 2 | 4 | 6 | 8 | 10 | 12 | 14 | 16 | 18 | 20 | 22 | 24 |
| 3 | 6 | 9 | 12 | 15 | 18 | 21 | 24 | 27 | 30 | 33 | 36 |
| 4 | 8 | 12 | 16 | 20 | 24 | 28 | 32 | 36 | 40 | 44 | 48 |
| 5 | 10 | 15 | 20 | 25 | 30 | 35 | 40 | 45 | 50 | 55 | 60 |
| 6 | 12 | 18 | 24 | 30 | 36 | 42 | 48 | 54 | 60 | 66 | 72 |
| 7 | 14 | 21 | 28 | 35 | 42 | 49 | 56 | 63 | 70 | 77 | 84 |
| 8 | 16 | 24 | 32 | 40 | 48 | 56 | 64 | 72 | 80 | 88 | 96 |
| 9 | 18 | 27 | 36 | 45 | 54 | 63 | 72 | 81 | 90 | 99 | 108 |
| 10 | 20 | 30 | 40 | 50 | 60 | 70 | 80 | 90 | 100 | 110 | 120 |
| 11 | 22 | 33 | 44 | 55 | 66 | 77 | 88 | 99 | 110 | 121 | 132 |
| 12 | 24 | 36 | 48 | 60 | 72 | 84 | 96 | 108 | 120 | 132 | 144 |

| 1 | 2 | 3 | 4 | 5 | 6 | 7 | 8 | 9 | 10 | 11 | 12 |
|---|---|---|---|---|---|---|---|---|---|---|---|
| 2 | 4 | 6 | 8 | 10 | 12 | 14 | 16 | 18 | 20 | 22 | 24 |
| 3 | 6 | 9 | 12 | 15 | 18 | 21 | 24 | 27 | 30 | 33 | 36 |
| 4 | 8 | 12 | 16 | 20 | 24 | 28 | 32 | 36 | 40 | 44 | 48 |
| 5 | 10 | 15 | 20 | 25 | 30 | 35 | 40 | 45 | 50 | 55 | 60 |
| 6 | 12 | 18 | 24 | 30 | 36 | 42 | 48 | 54 | 60 | 66 | 72 |
| 7 | 14 | 21 | 28 | 35 | 42 | 49 | 56 | 63 | 70 | 77 | 84 |
| 8 | 16 | 24 | 32 | 40 | 48 | 56 | 64 | 72 | 80 | 88 | 96 |
| 9 | 18 | 27 | 36 | 45 | 54 | 63 | 72 | 81 | 90 | 99 | 108 |
| 10 | 20 | 30 | 40 | 50 | 60 | 70 | 80 | 90 | 100 | 110 | 120 |
| 11 | 22 | 33 | 44 | 55 | 66 | 77 | 88 | 99 | 110 | 121 | 132 |
| 12 | 24 | 36 | 48 | 60 | 72 | 84 | 96 | 108 | 120 | 132 | 144 |

*Observing multiplication and division patterns*

# Perfecting Perimeter!

*"Ant-icipate" a fun time with this lesson about measuring perimeter!*

**Skills:** Using a metric ruler to find perimeter; solving problems about perimeter

**Estimated Lesson Time:** 45 minutes

## Teacher Preparation:
1. Duplicate one copy of the reproducible on page 37 for each student.
2. On a blank transparency, draw five irregular polygons with any number of sides. Make the length of each side a whole number.

## Materials:
1 copy of page 37 for each student
1 centimeter ruler for each student
1 blank transparency
1 transparency pen
an overhead projector

Perimeter is the distance around a polygon.

## Background Information:
*Perimeter* is the distance around a polygon. The perimeter of a polygon is found by adding together the lengths of its sides.

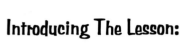

## Introducing The Lesson:

Draw the polygons below on your chalkboard without labeling their measurements. Explain that these polygons represent drawings of three different playgrounds. Ask your students how they could determine the distance around each playground (*measure the sides of each polygon with a customary or metric ruler*). Next point to each polygon in turn and ask what the distance around that shape is called (*perimeter*). Then remind your students how to find perimeter (see page 35).

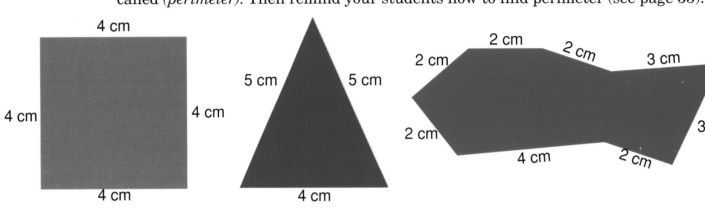

## Steps:

1. Demonstrate how to find the perimeter of each polygon on the board. In turn, measure and record the lengths of each polygon's sides; then add the measurements to find each perimeter. If desired, use the formulas below to show your steps.

   | | | |
   |---|---|---|
   | P = s + s + s + s | P = s + s + s | P = s + s + s + s + s + s + s + s |
   | P = 4 + 4 + 4 + 4 | P = 4 + 5 + 5 | P = 2 + 2 + 2 + 2 + 3 + 3 + 2 + 4 |
   | P = 16 cm | P = 14 cm | P = 20 cm |

2. Display the transparency that you created on an overhead projector. Demonstrate how to measure each side of the first polygon with a centimeter ruler. Then find the perimeter of this polygon by adding together its measurements.

3. Next have a student come up to the overhead. Direct him to use the same ruler to measure the sides of one of the other polygons. Then instruct him to determine its perimeter by adding together its measurements.

4. Select three more students, in turn, to measure and find the perimeters of the three remaining polygons.

5. Afterward give each student a centimeter ruler and one copy of page 37 for more practice in measuring with metric rulers.

# Mrs. Carpenter's Ants

Mrs. Carpenter teaches the fourth grade at Anthill Academy. To teach her students about measuring perimeter, she asked every ant to measure his yard as if he were going to enclose it with a fence.

Look at the map below that shows the shape of each ant's yard. Use this diagram and a centimeter ruler to find the perimeter of each yard. Then work the problems at the bottom of the page.

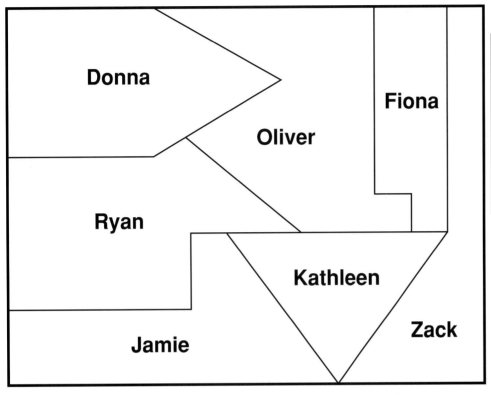

Perimeter is the distance around a polygon.

1. The perimeter of Donna's yard:
   P = _____ cm

2. The perimeter of Oliver's yard:
   P = _____ cm

3. The perimeter of Fiona's yard:
   P = _____ cm

4. The perimeter of Ryan's yard:
   P = _____ cm

5. The perimeter of Jamie's yard:
   P = _____ cm

6. The perimeter of Kathleen's yard:
   P = _____ cm

7. The perimeter of Zack's yard:
   P = _____ cm

8. What is the perimeter of the rectangular map above? _____ cm

9. Whose yard has the greatest perimeter? _____ The smallest perimeter?_____

10. If a fence costs $1.50 per centimeter, how much would it cost each ant to enclose his yard with a fence? (Pretend that each ant's yard is separate and does not border a neighbor's yard.) Write the cost of each ant's fence underneath his name on the diagram above.

> **Bonus Box:** Find the cost of a fence at $1.50 per centimeter that completely encloses the neighborhood and separates each ant's yard. (Hint: Only one fence is needed between two neighboring yards.)

(37)

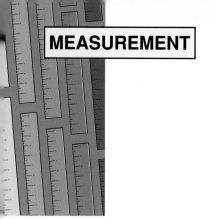
## How To Extend The Lesson:

• Have your students use trundle wheels or measuring tapes to measure the perimeter of your playground. Afterward direct them to figure the cost of enclosing this area with a fence, using a quoted price from your local hardware store. If a fence already exists at your school, have your students compute its cost at the recently quoted price.

• For homework, give each student a tape measure to use to measure the perimeter of her bedroom. Then have her find the cost of redecorating the walls of her room with wallpaper border. Give her more than one choice for purchasing the border she'll need. For example, allow her to buy individual rolls of a given length at a set price or double rolls of a given length at a higher price. Instruct her to list the exact number of rolls she'll need and their total cost on paper.

• Challenge your students to draw and label the six different ways of creating a garden with a perimeter of 24 feet *(1' x 11', 2' x 10', 3' x 9', 4' x 8', 5' x 7', and 6' x 6').*

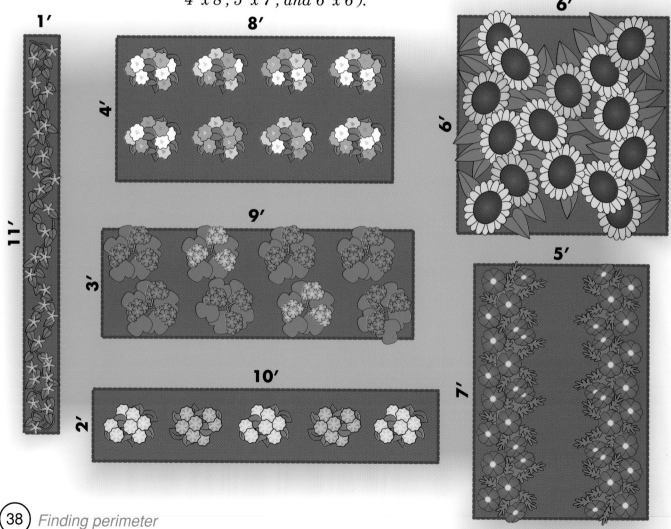

# An Area Of Expertise!

*Turn your students into experts on finding
area with the following hands-on activities!*

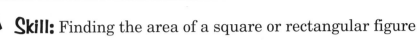

**Skill:** Finding the area of a square or rectangular figure

**Estimated Lesson Time:** 45 minutes

## Teacher Preparation:

1. Draw the two squares and two rectangles shown on page 40 on a blank transparency. (Do not include the measurements.)
2. Make one transparency of a blank centimeter-grid square.
3. Duplicate a blank centimeter-grid square for each student.
4. Duplicate one copy of page 41 for each student.

## Materials:

2 blank overhead transparencies
1 overhead marking pen
1 centimeter ruler for each student
1 copy of a blank centimeter-grid square for each student
1 copy of page 41 for each student

## Background Information:

The area of a square or rectangular figure is the number of square units within the surface of that figure. Area is measured in square units—such as square meters, centimeters, or millimeters. The area of a square or rectangular figure is found by either counting the number of square units within that figure or by multiplying the length of that figure by its width.

The formula for finding the area of a square or rectangular figure is Area = length x width *(A = l x w).*

**Example:**

l = 4 cm
w = 3 cm
Area = 12 square
cm

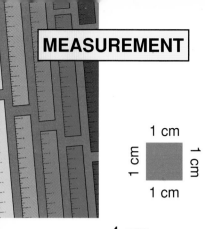

1 cm

1 cm | | 1 cm

1 cm

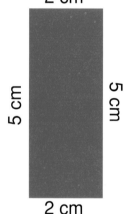

4 cm

3 cm | | 3 cm

4 cm

A = l x w
A = 4 cm x 3 cm
A = 12 square cm

2 cm

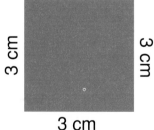

5 cm | | 5 cm

2 cm

A = l x w
A = 5 cm x 2 cm
A = 10 square cm

3 cm

3 cm | | 3 cm

3 cm

A = l x w
A = 3 cm x 3 cm
A = 9 square cm

## Introducing The Lesson:

Display the transparency of the squares and rectangles created earlier on an overhead projector. Point out the single square centimeter to your students. Then ask how many square centimeters it would take to fill the inside of each rectangle if the squares were placed in neat rows side by side. *(Students will probably tell you to draw rows of square centimeters inside each figure and count them.)* Place the centimeter-grid transparency over each figure on the rectangular-shapes transparency, in turn. Have a different student volunteer count the number of square centimeters in each figure and record it as square centimeters next to that figure.

## Steps:

1. Explain to your students that they just determined the area of each rectangle by counting the number of squares in each figure. Share the background information on page 39 with your students, explaining that using a formula is another way to find the area of a square or rectangle.

2. Use a metric ruler to measure and record the length and width of each rectangle on the transparency. Then demonstrate how to find the area of each rectangle by using the formula $A = l \; x \; w$.

3. Next give each student one sheet of centimeter-grid paper. Direct each student to draw a rectangle with a length of 5 centimeters and a width of 6 centimeters on her grid paper while you do the same on the centimeter-grid transparency.

4. After each student has drawn the rectangle, have her use the formula to find the area of it *(5 cm x 6 cm = 30 square cm)*. Then have each student count the number of centimeter squares inside her rectangle to confirm the answer. Afterward record the correct answer on the transparency.

5. Next have each student draw any two rectangles no greater than five squares in length or width on her paper. Direct the student to trade her paper with a classmate. Have the classmate use the formula $A = l \; x \; w$ to find the area of each rectangle and confirm the answers by counting the number of squares inside each figure.

6. Give each student a copy of page 41. Instruct each student to follow the directions on the reproducible to complete the activity. Afterward discuss the answers together as a class.

# The Lady's An Expert!

Linda Ladybug is an expert on finding area. She often has to cover a lot of territory in order to find food. Linda's busy helping the young ladies from the local Ladybug Garden Club learn how to find the area of a square or rectangular figure. She's divided a diagram of a garden into eight different sections.

Look at the diagram below that shows the outline of each section. Use a centimeter ruler to measure the length and width of each section; then use the formula shown to find the area of each section. Record your answers in the blanks next to each number.

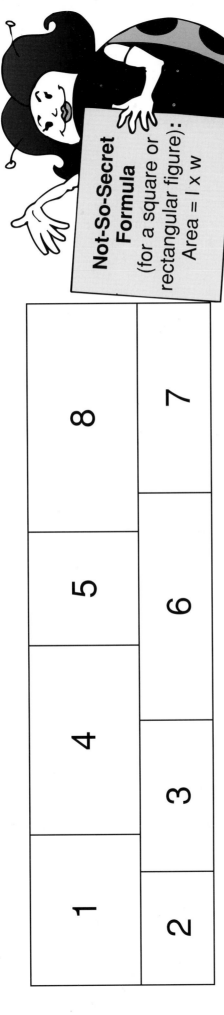

**Not-So-Secret Formula**
(for a square or rectangular figure):
Area = l x w

1.  l = _____  w = _____
    Area = _____ square cm

2.  l = _____  w = _____
    Area = _____ square cm

3.  l = _____  w = _____
    Area = _____ square cm

4.  l = _____  w = _____
    Area = _____ square cm

5.  l = _____  w = _____
    Area = _____ square cm

6.  l = _____  w = _____
    Area = _____ square cm

7.  l = _____  w = _____
    Area = _____ square cm

8.  l = _____  w = _____
    Area = _____ square cm

9.  Which section has the greatest area? _____
    Which has the smallest area? _____

10. If the ladybugs find one aphid to munch on in each square centimeter of the garden, how many aphids will they find in all? _____

**Bonus Box:** If the width of section #3 changed from 2 cm to 4 cm, by how many square centimeters would the area of the square change?

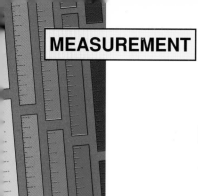
## How To Extend The Lesson:

- Direct each student to bring in a household item to measure with—such as a soup can, a cereal box, or a book. Divide your students into groups of four; then have each group first estimate and then measure the length and width of your classroom using each member's item. Next have the group use those measurements to calculate your classroom's area. Point out to each group that its measurements should be recorded in nonstandard units because of the items used. For example, if your classroom measured 20 cereal boxes by 20 cereal boxes, its area would be recorded as 400 square cereal-box units. Finally give each group a metric ruler for finding the actual area of your classroom in square centimeters. Afterward discuss each group's findings as a class.

- Have each student find the area of her bedroom. Direct the student to use a ruler or measuring tape to measure the length and width of her room to the nearest centimeter. Then have her use the formula $A = l \times w$ to calculate the area of her room in square centimeters.

- Give each student a blank sheet of centimeter-grid paper. Direct each student to draw and color the squares on his grid paper to create a picture of an object or figure—such as a flower, an animal, or a hot-air balloon. After each student completes his picture, instruct him to estimate its area. Then have the student count the actual number of squares to check the accuracy of his estimate. Finally direct each student to exchange his paper with a classmate to check it for accuracy before sharing both his picture and calculation with the class.

The flower has an area of 62 square cm.

# Time Out For Time!

*Your students will score big with this winning, time-measurement activity!*

**Skill:** Finding elapsed time

**Estimated Lesson Time:** 45 minutes

## Teacher Preparation:
1. Duplicate a copy of a Saturday listing from a television guide.
2. Make an overhead transparency of the television listing.
3. Copy your class's daily schedule onto a sheet of chart paper. See Step 1 on page 44.
4. Duplicate one copy of page 45 for each student.

## Materials:
1 Saturday listing from a television guide
1 overhead transparency
1 sheet of chart paper
1 marker
1 copy of page 45 for each student

It may be necessary to give students practice in renaming increments of time—such as 60 seconds = 1 minute, 60 minutes = 1 hour, 126 minutes = 2 hours and 6 minutes, etc.

## Background Information:
To find the elapsed time for two given times that are less than one hour apart, count the number of minutes in manageable increments from the first time to get as close as possible to the second time. For example, to find the elapsed time between 9:13 A.M. and 10:02 A.M., think: 9:13 to 9:15 is 2 minutes, 9:15 to 10:00 is 45 minutes, and 10:00 to 10:02 is 2 minutes. So the elapsed time is 2 minutes + 45 minutes + 2 minutes = 49 minutes.

To find the elapsed time for two given times that are one hour or more apart, count the number of hours from the first time to get as close as possible to the second time; then count the number of minutes in manageable increments to get to the second time. For example, to find the elapsed time between 11:20 A.M. and 1:35 P.M., think: 11:20 to 1:20 is 2 hours, and 1:20 to 1:35 is 15 minutes. So the elapsed time is 2 hours and 15 minutes.

## Introducing The Lesson:

Position the transparency you created on an overhead projector. In turn, point to a TV show on the transparency that lasts for 30 minutes, 1 hour, and more than 1 hour, each time asking the following questions: "How long does _____ last?" and "How do you know the show lasts that long?" *(by calculating the amount of time that elapses between the beginning and ending times listed)* Explain to students how to calculate elapsed time using the Background Information on page 43. Next have each student choose any TV program listed on the transparency and calculate how long the program lasts.

## Steps:

1. Write your class's daily schedule on a sheet of chart paper in four columns: Subject/Activity, Starting Time, Length In Minutes, and Ending Time. Fill in the first, second, and fourth columns for the class. Leave the third column blank.

2. Pair each student with a partner and have each pair calculate the length in hours and/or minutes of each subject or activity.

3. Check your students' answers together as a class. Have a different volunteer record the correct elapsed time for each subject or activity on the chart. Then ask your students questions such as the ones listed below:

- How much time passes between the starting and ending times of our first and second subjects or activities?
- In which subject or activity are you participating when it is 35 minutes after 9:15 A.M.?
- How much time passes between our scheduled math and science classes?
- In which subject or activity are you participating when it is 1 hour and 30 minutes after lunch?
- How much time passes from the time school begins until you leave school at the end of the day?

4. Give each student a copy of page 45. Instruct each student to follow the directions on the reproducible to complete the activity. After students have completed the activity, discuss the answers as a class.

# Keeping Track Of Time

Harry Hare, the coach of the Lickety-Split Track Team, has to get his group into shape in time for their big meet! Harry likes to keep track of how much time each team member spends in training each day. Work each problem on the back of this sheet; then record your answer on the line provided.

1.  Sunburst Sally started weight training 16 minutes after her 7:45 A.M. breakfast and stopped at 10:10 A.M. _____

2.  Wildfire Willy raced Streakin' Sam from 20 minutes before 8:00 A.M. to 13 minutes after 9:00 A.M. _____

3.  From 2 hours and 15 minutes before 11:00 A.M. until noon, Lightning Larry ran laps around the track. _____

4.  After jumping rope for an hour, Jumpin' Jane walked from 3:25 P.M. until 4 hours and 22 minutes after noon. _____

5.  It was from a quarter to 1:00 P.M. until an hour earlier than 4:45 P.M. that Hasty Hal worked on jumping over hurdles. _____

6.  Speedy Reedy sprinted from 5 minutes after 11:40 A.M. until 2 minutes after one o'clock in the afternoon. _____

7.  Inna Flash starting jogging at 3:50 P.M. and stopped at 10 minutes before 5:10 P.M. _____

8.  Twinkling Tammy started tumbling at 3:38 P.M. and ended halfway between noon and midnight. _____

9.  Pronto Paula took an early-morning walk from 5:18 A.M. until 3 minutes after 6:00 A.M. _____

10. Bounding Byron swam laps in the pool from 11:55 A.M. until 1 hour and 10 minutes after 2:35 P.M. _____

11. Chop-Chop Charo took a step aerobics class from 10:45 A.M. to 12:12 P.M. _____

12. Rapid Ron ran on the treadmill from 3 hours and 20 minutes before 2:20 P.M. until 11:35 A.M. _____

13. Pacing Pete worked out in the gym from 2:10 P.M. to 5:16 P.M. _____

14. Runabout Ralph put in a long day. He trained from 6:30 A.M. until 2:47 P.M. _____

**Bonus Box:** Find the total time that Wildfire Willy, Inna Flash, and Runabout Ralph spent in training.

(45)

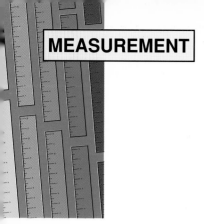

## How To Extend The Lesson:

- Have each student record a schedule of his activities from the time he awakes in the morning until the time he goes to bed at night. On the following school day, direct each student to determine the amount of time he spent on each activity. Next have him trade papers with a partner, check his partner's answers for accuracy, and ask him five questions similar to those listed in Step 3 on page 44.

- Gather one index card for each student. On half of the cards, label a period of time such as "7:15 A.M. to 9:35 A.M." On the other half of the cards, record the elapsed time to match each of the time-period cards. Next mix the cards, and have each student choose one card. Direct each student with a time-period card to calculate the elapsed time. Then, at your signal, have each of those students find a classmate who has the matching elapsed-time card. After all the matches have been made, collect the cards and mix them again. Begin another round by having each student choose a new card.

- Direct each student to imagine that she is in charge of planning the next class field trip, explaining that the class should arrive at the chosen place at 10:00 A.M. and leave at 3:30 P.M. Write the table shown below on the board; then give each student a 4" x 6" index card. Instruct each student to prepare a field-trip itinerary that includes an event and a time period for each amount of elapsed time listed on the table (see the example). Have each student share her itinerary; then display each one on a wall or bulletin board titled "Time For A Fabulous Field Trip!"

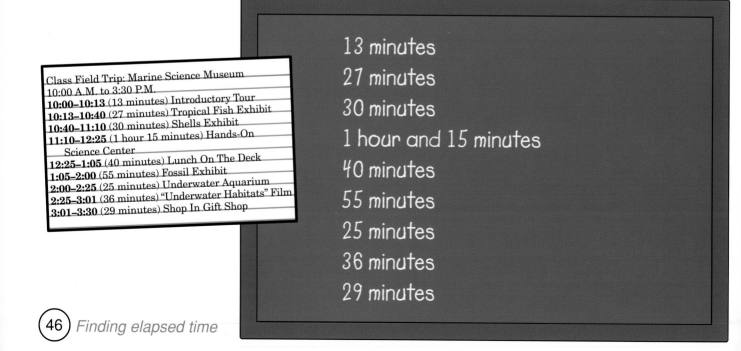

Class Field Trip: Marine Science Museum
10:00 A.M. to 3:30 P.M.
**10:00–10:13** (13 minutes) Introductory Tour
**10:13–10:40** (27 minutes) Tropical Fish Exhibit
**10:40–11:10** (30 minutes) Shells Exhibit
**11:10–12:25** (1 hour 15 minutes) Hands-On
    Science Center
**12:25–1:05** (40 minutes) Lunch On The Deck
**1:05–2:00** (55 minutes) Fossil Exhibit
**2:00–2:25** (25 minutes) Underwater Aquarium
**2:25–3:01** (36 minutes) "Underwater Habitats" Film
**3:01–3:30** (29 minutes) Shop In Gift Shop

13 minutes

27 minutes

30 minutes

1 hour and 15 minutes

40 minutes

55 minutes

25 minutes

36 minutes

29 minutes

# A Day At The Zoo

*Help your students tame problem solving with this lesson*
*on making and using a table!*

**Skill:** Making and using a table

**Estimated Lesson Time:** 45 minutes

### Teacher Preparation:
1. Duplicate one copy of page 49 for each student.
2. Make a transparency of page 49.
3. Make a transparency of the two problems at the bottom of page 50.

### Materials:
1 copy of page 49 for each student
2 blank transparencies
overhead projector pen

| Day | 1 | 2 | 3 | 4 | 5 | 6 | 7 |
|---|---|---|---|---|---|---|---|
| Lion | | | | | | | |
| Monkey | | | | | | | |

### Background Information:
Problem solvers who use the strategy of making tables can easily organize data, spot patterns, and identify missing information.

## Introducing The Lesson:

Begin this lesson by asking students which problem-solving strategies they have learned this year. Possible answers can include *logical reasoning, drawing a picture, acting it out or using objects, working backwards, making an organized list, guessing and checking, looking for a pattern,* and *making it simpler.* Inform your students that they will be learning a new problem-solving strategy in this lesson called *making and using a table.*

### Steps:

1. Display the transparency that you created earlier of the problems at the bottom of page 50. Then read the first problem on the transparency aloud.

2. Demonstrate how to solve the problem by making a table and filling it out as shown below.

| Seats | 1 | 2 | 3 | 4 | 5 | 6 | 7 | 8 | 9 | 10 | 11 | 12 | 13 | 14 | 15 | 16 | 17 | 18 | 19 | 20 | 21 |
|---|---|---|---|---|---|---|---|---|---|---|---|---|---|---|---|---|---|---|---|---|---|
| Empty | | | X | | | X | | | X | | | X | | | X | | | X | | | X |
| Occupied | X | X | | X | X | | X | X | | X | X | | X | X | | X | X | | X | X | |

*(Solution: There are 14 occupied seats on the tram.)*

3. Read the second problem aloud and again demonstrate how to make a table to solve the problem (see the table below).

| Day | 1 | 2 | 3 | 4 | 5 | 6 | 7 | 8 | 9 | 10 | 11 | 12 | 13 | 14 |
|---|---|---|---|---|---|---|---|---|---|---|---|---|---|---|
| Ticket Window | | X | | X | | X | | X | | X | | X | | X |
| Monkey Costume | | | X | | | X | | | X | | | X | | |

*(Solution: Colin will work the ticket window dressed as a monkey twice in a two-week period.)*

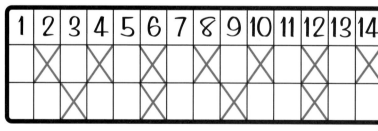

4. Distribute one copy of page 49 to each student and instruct him to complete it as directed. Afterward, use the transparency you created of page 49 to go over the correct solution to each problem.

Name _____

# A Day At The Zoo

Solve each of the problems below, using the make-a-table strategy.

1. Shana helps feed the animals at the zoo. Every third day she gets to feed the monkeys, and every sixth day she gets to feed the elephants. How many times will she get to feed the monkeys and the elephants on the same day during a three-week period?

| Day | 1 | 2 | 3 | 4 | 5 | 6 | 7 | 8 | 9 | 10 | 11 | 12 | 13 | 14 | 15 | 16 | 17 | 18 | 19 | 20 | 21 |
|---|---|---|---|---|---|---|---|---|---|---|---|---|---|---|---|---|---|---|---|---|---|
| Monkeys | | | | | | | | | | | | | | | | | | | | | |
| Elephants | | | | | | | | | | | | | | | | | | | | | |

Solution: _____

2. Josh and his friend CJ both work at the zoo. The boys are working together today, but they have different work schedules. Josh works every other day, and CJ works every third day. How many days will they both be working at the zoo on the same day during the next two weeks?

| Day | | | | | | | | | | | | |
|---|---|---|---|---|---|---|---|---|---|---|---|---|
| Josh | | | | | | | | | | | | |
| CJ | | | | | | | | | | | | |

Solution: _____

3. Cheryl was put in charge of the snack bar. She noticed that every third person bought a drink, every fourth person bought pizza, and every sixth person bought ice cream. If 30 people visited the snack bar, how many bought ice cream and a drink (but no pizza)? How many bought all three items?

| Customer | 1 | | | | 5 | | | | | 10 | | | | | 15 |
|---|---|---|---|---|---|---|---|---|---|---|---|---|---|---|---|
| Drink | | | | | | | | | | | | | | | |
| Pizza | | | | | | | | | | | | | | | |
| Ice Cream | | | | | | | | | | | | | | | |

| Customer | 16 | | | | 20 | | | | | 25 | | | | | 30 |
|---|---|---|---|---|---|---|---|---|---|---|---|---|---|---|---|
| Drink | | | | | | | | | | | | | | | |
| Pizza | | | | | | | | | | | | | | | |
| Ice Cream | | | | | | | | | | | | | | | |

Solution: _____

**Bonus Box:** In problem two above, how many days will Josh and CJ be working together during the next six weeks?

## How To Extend The Lesson:

- For additional practice with this problem-solving strategy, have students solve the two problems below.

1. Sharon walks to her job at the zoo. On her walk, she sees her neighbor every third day and her cousin every seventh day. How many times during a six-week period will Sharon see both her neighbor and her cousin on the same day?
   *(Sharon will see her neighbor and her cousin on the same day once in three weeks; therefore, she will see them twice in six weeks.)*

2. Jamaal spends twice as much time working at the bear exhibit than he does at the giraffe exhibit. One week, he worked a total of 24 hours at the two exhibits. How many hours did he spend at the giraffe exhibit?
   *(Jamaal spent eight hours at the giraffe exhibit.)*

- Give your students additional problems that can be solved using the make-a-table strategy, but require that least common multiples be used for all solutions. For example, suppose that Shana feeds the monkeys every third day and the elephants every sixth day. Also suppose that she wants to know how many times during a 21-day period she will feed both the monkeys and the elephants on the same day. Your students can determine that since the LCM of 3 and 6 is 6, Shana will feed both animal groups every day that is a multiple of 6. Therefore, Shana will feed the monkeys and elephants three times in 21 days—on the 6th day (6 x 1 = 6), the 12th day (6 x 2 = 12), and on the 18th day (6 x 3 = 18). Not only will your students receive more practice with LCMs, but they will learn that there is more than one way to solve a problem.

1. **Mrs. May noticed that every third seat on the tram was empty. If she counted 21 seats on the tram, how many of those seats were filled?**

| 1 | 2 | 3 | 4 | 5 | 6 | 7 | 8 | 9 | 10 | 11 | 12 | 13 | 14 | 15 | 16 | 17 | 18 | 19 | 20 | 21 |
|---|---|---|---|---|---|---|---|---|----|----|----|----|----|----|----|----|----|----|----|----|
|   |   |   |   |   |   |   |   |   |    |    |    |    |    |    |    |    |    |    |    |    |

2. **Colin got a job at the zoo. Every other day he works at the ticket window, and every third day he dresses as a monkey. If Colin works a seven-day week, how many days in two weeks will he have to work the ticket window dressed as a monkey?**

| 1 | 2 | 3 | 4 | 5 | 6 | 7 | 8 | 9 | 10 | 11 | 12 | 13 | 14 |
|---|---|---|---|---|---|---|---|---|----|----|----|----|----|
|   |   |   |   |   |   |   |   |   |    |    |    |    |    |

# Let Go And Guess!

*Swing into problem solving with the greatest of ease
with this guess-and-check lesson!*

**Skill:** Using the guess-and-check technique to solve math problems

**Estimated Lesson Time:** 45 minutes

## Teacher Preparation:
1. Duplicate one copy of page 53 for each student.
2. Copy the six guess-and-check problems from "Introducing The Lesson" on page 52 on the board.

## Materials:
1 copy of page 53 for each student
1 sheet of 6" x 15" construction paper for each student
1 pair of scissors for each student
1 marker for each student
1 ruler for each student

## Background Information:
The guess-and-check method of problem solving involves guessing the answer to a problem, and then checking to see if the guess is correct. If that guess is incorrect, another more reasonable guess is made, continuing in this manner until a solution is reached. Many guess-and-check problems have more than one solution. Guessing and checking is especially useful when a problem contains several pieces of data.

39!

The ones-place digit of my two-digit number is three times its tens-place digit. If the digits in my number are added together, the ones-place digit is twice its tens-place digit. What's my number?

*Using guess and check* (51)

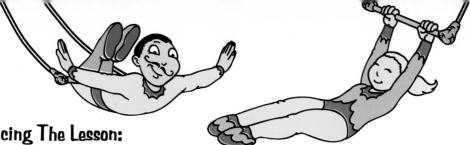

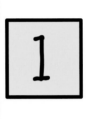

## Introducing The Lesson:

Begin by asking students how they would solve the problems on the board. Explain that since there are several possible solutions to each problem, the guess-and-check method of problem solving can be used. Point out that the guess-and-check method involves guessing a solution, and then checking to see if the guess is correct. Point out that each incorrect guess provides valuable information that can be used in formulating the next guess. Work the first problem on the board using the guess-and-check method. Discuss each step of the process as you work toward the solution.

1.
```
  ☐☐
+ ☐☐
-----
  7 5
```
2.
```
  ☐☐
- ☐☐
-----
  4 1
```
3.
```
  ☐☐
x  ☐
-----
  7 8
```
4.
```
   ☐☐☐
+  ☐☐☐
------
  4 6 7
```
5.
```
  ☐4
x  ☐
-----
 3☐0
```
6.
```
   ☐
  ☐☐
+ ☐☐
-----
  9 7
```

Possible answers: *(Note: Other answers are possible. Accept all correct solutions.)*

1.
```
  1 2
+ 6 3
-----
  7 5
```
2.
```
  6 9
- 2 8
-----
  4 1
```
3.
```
  1 3
x   6
-----
  7 8
```
4.
```
  3 5 8
+ 1 0 9
-------
  4 6 7
```
5.
```
  6 4
x   5
-----
 3 2 0
```
6.
```
    1
  4 6
+ 5 0
-----
  9 7
```

## Steps:

1. Give each student a sheet of 6" x 15" construction paper. Then direct the student to measure and cut out ten 3" x 3" paper squares.

2. Have each student write a different number from zero to nine on each square.

3. Direct each student to manipulate her number squares to come up with a possible solution to the second problem on the board. Then have her check her answer. Encourage each student to continue to guess and check until a solution is reached. Discuss the solution to problem number two.

4. Repeat this procedure for problems three through six. Remind students that there may be more than one correct solution for each problem.

5. Challenge each student to make up a problem similar to those on the board to share with the class.

6. Give each student a copy of page 53 for additional practice with the guess-and-check method of problem solving.

# Swing Into Problem Solving

The guess-and-check problem-solving method will help you solve the circus problems below with the greatest of ease. Read each problem, guess its answer, and then check your answer. Continue guessing and checking until you make a correct guess. Remember, there may be more than one correct answer for each problem.

## Circus Snack Bar
## (Prices Include Tax)

| FOOD | | | | BEVERAGES | |
|---|---|---|---|---|---|
| Gum | $.45 | Nachos | $2.00 | Hot Chocolate | $1.00 |
| Candy Bar | $.75 | Soft Pretzel | $1.45 | Iced Tea | $1.35 |
| Popcorn | $1.50 | Corn Dog | $1.25 | Soft Drink | $1.75 |
| Cotton Candy | $1.25 | Chili Dog | $3.25 | | |
| Peanuts | $.50 | Ice Cream | $1.65 | | |

**Directions:** Answer the following questions using the information on the menu board of the Circus Snack Bar.

1. If you spent $10.00 on five items at the Circus Snack Bar, what did you buy?
_____

2. If your brother spent $7.35 at the Circus Snack Bar, what did he buy?
_____

3. If Hannah, the tightrope walker, spent less than $1.00 on two items at the snack bar, what did she buy? _____

4. If Calvin, the clown, bought a beverage and a snack for $1.50, which items did he buy?
_____

5. If Tommy, the lion tamer, bought three beverages and three snacks with only $7.50, what did he buy?
_____

6. If Tanya, the trapeze artist, bought two beverages and three snacks for $6.75, what did she buy?

**Directions:** Using four darts, what score combinations could Daredevil Dan have come up with to earn the scores below?

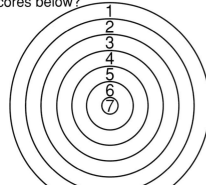

7. Score of 16: dart 1 _____ dart 2 _____ dart 3 _____ dart 4 _____

8. Score of 10: dart 1 _____ dart 2 _____ dart 3 _____ dart 4 _____

9. Score of 25: dart 1 _____ dart 2 _____ dart 3 _____ dart 4 _____

10. Score of 17: dart 1 _____ dart 2 _____ dart 3 _____ dart 4 _____

11. Score of 21: dart 1 _____ dart 2 _____ dart 3 _____ dart 4 _____

12. Score of 18: dart 1 _____ dart 2 _____ dart 3 _____ dart 4 _____

**Bonus Box:** Make up three additional problems using the dartboard above. Then give your problems to a classmate to solve.

## How To Extend The Lesson:

- Randomly open any textbook and call out the odd page number that is visible. Challenge each student to use the guess-and-check method to find two consecutive pages in the book whose sum equals the page number you announced. For example, if you called out page 13, page numbers 6 and 7 would equal that sum. After calling out several simple number combinations, gradually work toward more complex ones.

- For additional guess-and-check practice, have each student roll a pair of dice three times and then record the sum of those three numbers. For example, if a student rolls a *4, 6,* and *3,* respectively, the sum of these numbers would be *13.* Instruct each student to give the sum of his numbers to a classmate who should use the guess-and-check method to find which three pairs of numbers from the dice add together to equal that sum *(1 + 3, 2 + 4, and 2 + 1 is one possible solution).* Remind each student that there may be more than one correct answer to each problem. To make the game more interesting, either increase the number of rolls, or have each student supply the guessing classmate with a helpful clue, such as "None of the numbers were repeated in each roll, and no throw was higher than four."

- Using removable labels, assign a different dollar amount to several objects located around your classroom. Give each student a different dollar amount, making sure that the amount you assign can be obtained by adding together some combination of the labeled items. Also assign each student a specific number of items to buy. Have each student then use the guess-and-check method to solve the problem. Repeat this activity several times, each time providing the student with a new total to reach and a different number of items to purchase for each new round.

# Scoring With Logic!

*Your students will get a real kick out of this lesson
involving logical reasoning!*

**Skill:** Using logical reasoning to solve problems

**Estimated Lesson Time:** 45 minutes

## Teacher Preparation:

1.  Duplicate one copy of page 57 for each student.
2.  Copy the paragraph and clues in "Introducing The Lesson" on page 56 onto a blank transparency.

## Materials:

1 copy of page 57 for each child
1 blank transparency
overhead projector markers

## Background Information:

Logical reasoning is used in all types of problem solving. One method of logical reasoning involves having students construct a table or grid from data to classify and organize information. The information is often provided in the form of a series of clues or statements. Constructing a table helps students combine and organize facts so that a solution can be found.

## PROBLEM-SOLVING STRATEGIES

### Introducing The Lesson:

On the overhead, display the transparency that you created of the problem below. Direct your students to read the information; then ask them what organizer could make solving the problem easier. Guide your students to conclude that a table or grid could organize the data in the clues. Point out that tables help organize information in a way that is easy to read and understand.

**Problem:**

Leslie, Evan, Mike, and Stephanie went to the pizza parlor after school. Each person ordered a small pizza with one of the following toppings: pepperoni, sausage, mushrooms, and green peppers. The waitress forgot which pizza each child ordered. Use the clues below to find out.

**Clues:**
1. Evan is sitting across from the girl who ordered a mushroom pizza and the girl who ordered one with green peppers.
2. Mike does not like pepperoni.
3. Leslie does not like green peppers.

### Steps:

1.  Copy the 4 x 4 grid below on the transparency. Explain that the table will be used to sort the data in the clues.

|           | pepperoni | sausage | mushrooms | green peppers |
|-----------|-----------|---------|-----------|---------------|
| Leslie    |           |         |           |               |
| Evan      |           |         |           |               |
| Mike      |           |         |           |               |
| Stephanie |           |         |           |               |

2.  Emphasize that recording information in a table helps make a problem's solution clearer by ruling out possibilities and determining options.

3.  Have a student volunteer read the first clue aloud to the class. Mark a √ in a box of the table if there is a match and an *X* if there is not.

4.  Continue in the same manner with the other clues until all the table's squares have been marked with either a √ or an *X* as shown.

|           | pepperoni | sausage | mushrooms | green peppers |
|-----------|-----------|---------|-----------|---------------|
| Leslie    | X         | X       | √         | X             |
| Evan      | √         | X       | X         | X             |
| Mike      | X         | √       | X         | X             |
| Stephanie | X         | X       | X         | √             |

*Using logic*     5.Give each student a copy of page 57 for additional practice.

# Score With Logic!

**Directions:** Use the information below to solve each logic problem.

The players on the Atlantic Hurricanes soccer team want to attend summer soccer camp. The team members could not decide on a fund-raising idea, so each player chose his own way to earn money for camp tuition. Read the clues below to find out how each child earned his money. Mark the table with a √ if there is a match and an *X* if there is not.

**Clues:**

1. Andrew lives on the same street as the girl who chose to run a pet-grooming service and the girl who decided to wash cars.

2. Carrie did not wash cars.

3. Jake told his friends that he was allergic to fresh grass cuttings.

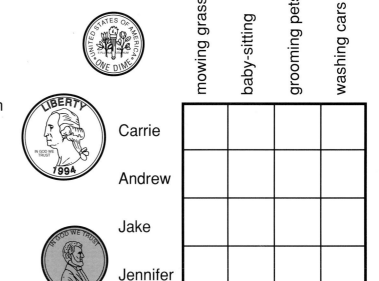

| | mowing grass | baby-sitting | grooming pets | washing cars |
|---|---|---|---|---|
| Carrie | | | | |
| Andrew | | | | |
| Jake | | | | |
| Jennifer | | | | |

Carrie, Andrew, Jake, and Jennifer each signed up to stay in a different cabin at the camp. Use the clues below to identify the cabin assignment for each camper. Mark a √ if there is a match and an *X* if there is not.

**Clues:**

1. Andrew and the girl staying in the Goalie Getaway are closer to the dining hall than the boy who is staying in the Halfback Hostel.

2. One of the girls is staying in the Defender's Den.

3. Carrie is not staying in the Defender's Den or the Sweeper Suite.

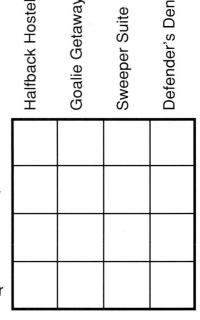

| | Halfback Hostel | Goalie Getaway | Sweeper Suite | Defender's Den |
|---|---|---|---|---|
| Carrie | | | | |
| Andrew | | | | |
| Jake | | | | |
| Jennifer | | | | |

**Bonus Box:** On the back of this sheet, use the same characters to develop a logic problem similar to the ones above. Then give your problem to a classmate to solve.

(57)

## How To Extend The Lesson:

- Record the following logic problem on the board and challenge your students to complete it independently:

    Madeline, Adrienne, Mackenzie, and Melody are all in the Girl Explorer Troop. Each girl is working to complete the requirements for earning a different badge—cooking, first aid, animal care, or recycling. Use the clues below to determine the badge each girl is working to earn.

**Clues:**

1. Madeline and Adrienne are not working on the cooking badge.
2. Mackenzie, Melody, and Adrienne go to the same school as the girl working on the animal-care badge.
3. Adrienne is not working on the first-aid badge.
4. Mackenzie already earned her badge in cooking.

|  | cooking | first aid | animal care | recycling |
|---|---|---|---|---|
| Madeline |  |  |  |  |
| Adrienne |  |  |  |  |
| Mackenzie |  |  |  |  |
| Melody |  |  |  |  |

### Answer:

|  | cooking | first aid | animal care | recycling |
|---|---|---|---|---|
| Madeline | X | X | ✓ | X |
| Adrienne | X | X | X | ✓ |
| Mackenzie | X | ✓ | X | X |
| Melody | ✓ | X | X | X |

- Have your students work together in teams to create a logic problem that involves using a table to find the solution. Provide each team with two copies of a simple 3 x 3 grid like the one below with which to organize its problem. Direct each group to label its grid with the necessary information and then record two to three clues below its grid. Have the group use the second grid to record the solution to its problem. Collect each group's problem and use it as a warm-up for an upcoming math lesson.

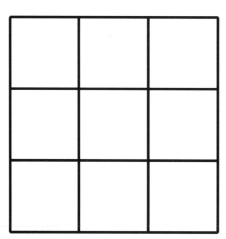

# A Problem-Solving Portrait

*Unveil a new problem-solving strategy—draw a picture.*

**Skill:** Drawing a picture or diagram to solve a problem

**Estimated Lesson Time:** 45 minutes

**Teacher Preparation:**
1. Duplicate one copy of page 61 for each student.
2. Make a transparency of the problem in Step 1 on page 60.

**Materials:**
1 copy of page 61 for each student
1 blank transparency
1 overhead marking pen

**Background Information:**
Sometimes it is helpful to use an available picture, or to draw a picture or diagram, when trying to solve a problem. The picture helps the problem solver understand and manipulate the data in the problem.

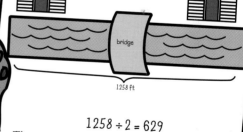

Kendra and Max live the same distance from the bridge. If they live 1,258 feet apart, how far does each one live from the bridge?

Max    Kendra

bridge

1258 ft

$1258 \div 2 = 629$
They each live 629 feet from the bridge.

## Introducing The Lesson:

Begin this lesson by asking students which problem-solving strategies they have learned this year. Possible answers can include *logical reasoning, making a table, acting it out or using objects, working backwards, making an organized list, guessing and checking, looking for a pattern,* and *making it simpler.* Inform your students that they will be learning a new problem-solving strategy in this lesson called *draw a picture or diagram.*

## Steps:

1.  Read aloud the problem below as you display the transparency that you created.

    Martin was halfway home from school on his 12-block walk when he realized that he forgot to stop at the store for milk. He walked back 3 blocks to the store, then continued his walk home. How many blocks from school is the store located? How many blocks did Martin walk in all?

2.  Explain to students that it is sometimes helpful to use an available picture or to draw a picture when trying to solve a problem. Demonstrate how to use a picture to solve this problem by re-creating the drawing below on the transparency as you read the problem aloud again.

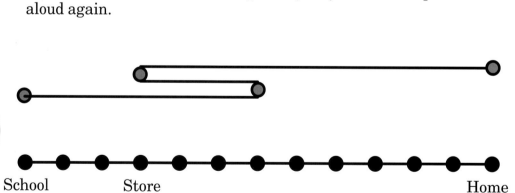

School        Store                                    Home

    *Solution: The store is located 3 blocks from the school, and Martin walked a total of 18 blocks in all.*

3.  Distribute one copy of page 61 to each student, and instruct him to complete the page as directed.

Name_____

# As Easel As 1, 2, 3!

Solve each problem below using the draw-a-picture strategy. Draw your picture on the easel provided for each problem. Then write your solution on the lines below each easel.

1. How many stamps are on the border of a 10 x 10 sheet of 100 stamps?

2. Farmer Ted has chickens and goats on his farm. He counted 28 legs and 9 heads on his animals out in the field. If each animal has one head and the correct number of legs, how many of each animal does Farmer Ted have?

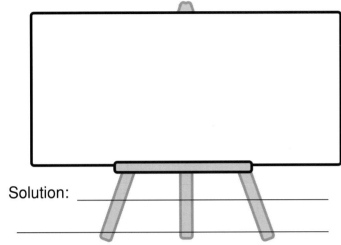

Solution: _____

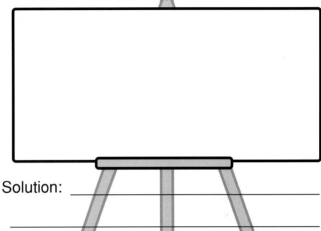

Solution: _____

3. Mrs. Foster's class went on a field trip to their state's capital. From the capitol building, the class walked six blocks north to the ice-cream shop, then four blocks west to the courthouse. They continued their tour by walking ten blocks south, then four blocks east to the museum. How far and in what direction does Mrs. Foster's class need to walk to get back to their bus that is parked in front of the capitol building?

4. Mrs. Lobasso's class is having races at recess to determine the fastest runner in the class. Two students race at a time, and the winner advances to the next round. Each student races until he loses. If there are 16 students in Mrs. Lobasso's class, how many races will it take to declare a winner?

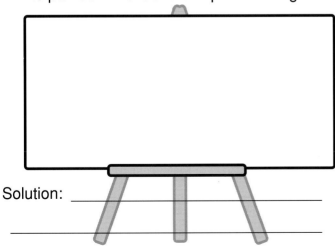

Solution: _____

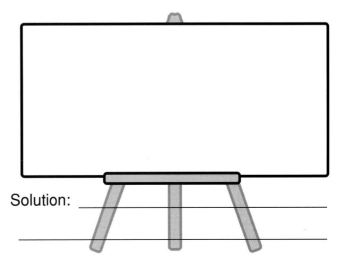

Solution: _____

**Bonus Box:** On the back of this sheet, draw a picture to solve problem number two if Farmer Ted had counted 38 legs and 13 heads in his field.

## How To Extend The Lesson:

- Give your students practice in using a picture by asking questions related to a calendar. For example, ask, "If May 5th is a Friday, what day will June 7th be?" *(June 7 will be a Wednesday.)*

| MAY | | | | | | |
|---|---|---|---|---|---|---|
| **S** | **M** | **T** | **W** | **T** | **F** | **S** |
| | 1 | 2 | 3 | 4 | ⑤ | 6 |
| 7 | 8 | 9 | 10 | 11 | 12 | 13 |
| 14 | 15 | 16 | 17 | 18 | 19 | 20 |
| 21 | 22 | 23 | 24 | 25 | 26 | 27 |
| 28 | 29 | 30 | 31 | | | |

| JUNE | | | | | | |
|---|---|---|---|---|---|---|
| **S** | **M** | **T** | **W** | **T** | **F** | **S** |
| | | | | | 1 | 2 | 3 |
| 4 | 5 | 6 | ⑦ | 8 | 9 | 10 |
| 11 | 12 | 13 | 14 | 15 | 16 | 17 |
| 18 | 19 | 20 | 21 | 22 | 23 | 24 |
| 25 | 26 | 27 | 28 | 29 | 30 | |

- Assign the following problems that can be solved by drawing a Venn diagram.

1. Ten boys are outside playing football. Seven are wearing hats, four are wearing coats, and three are wearing both hats and coats. How many boys are wearing neither hats nor coats?

   *(Two boys are wearing neither hats nor coats.)*

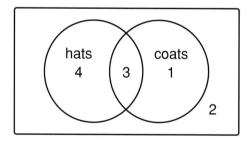

2. Of the 25 students in Mr. Giovani's class, 14 wear glasses, 18 have braces, and 8 wear glasses and have braces. How many students in Mr. Giovani's class wear only glasses?

   *(Six students in Mr. Giovani's class only wear glasses.)*

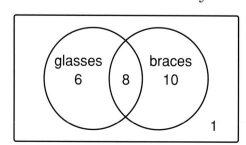

# A List Made To Order!

*Happy faces will be the order of the day with these fun problem-solving activities!*

**Skill:** Solving word problems using an organized list

**Estimated Lesson Time:** 45 minutes

## Teacher Preparation:

1. Duplicate four, different-colored smiley faces for each student using the pattern below.
2. Duplicate one copy of page 65 for each student.

## Materials:

4 different-colored smiley faces for each student
1 copy of page 65 for each student
paper and pencil for each student

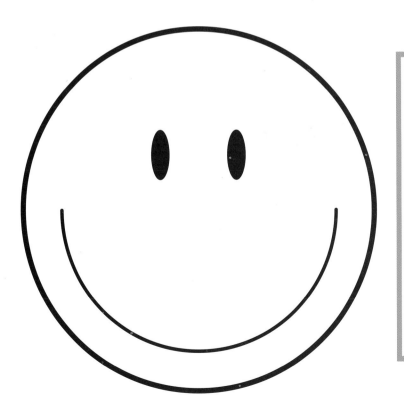

## Background Information:

Making an organized list is a very helpful strategy for students to use when solving some word problems. An organized list can be used when items need to be put in a given order or when all possible combinations of a group of items need to be known. Encourage the use of systematic listing to ensure that choices are not left out or repeated.

*Making an organized list* (63)

## Introducing The Lesson:

Direct three student volunteers to stand at the front of the classroom. Explain to the class that these volunteers are going to pose for an imaginary group photo. Ask the class how many different ways the three volunteers can be arranged in left-to-right order for the photo. Suggest that the class tell—and the volunteers act out—each arrangement beginning with the volunteer on the left. Systematically list each different arrangement on the board, continuing until all possible arrangements have been listed. *(Six combinations are possible: 1, 2, 3; 1, 3, 2; 2, 1, 3; 2, 3, 1; 3, 1, 2; and 3, 2, 1.)* Point out how making an organized list can show all the possible choices and ensure that choices are not left out or repeated.

## Steps:

1. Give each student four of the different-colored smiley faces that you duplicated earlier. Direct each student to systematically list all the possible ways the faces can be arranged in a left-to-right order on a sheet of loose-leaf paper. *(There are 24 different possible arrangements, six for each color smiley face. See the example below.)*

2. Pair your students; then have each partner check his partner's list.

3. Give each student a copy of page 65 and instruct him to follow its directions. After each student has completed the activity, discuss the answers together as a class.

| PRYO | RPOY | YPOR | OPRY |
| PROY | RPYO | YPRO | OPYR |
| PORY | ROYP | YROP | ORYP |
| POYR | ROPY | YRPO | ORPY |
| PYRO | RYPO | YORP | OYRP |
| PYOR | RYOP | YOPR | OYPR |

Name_____

# The Happy-Day Cafe!

Some of the students in Mrs. Smiley's class are having lunch at their favorite local cafe. As always, there are many combinations from which to choose! Look at the menu board shown below; then help each student determine all the possible combinations for solving each problem. Make an organized list for each problem on the back of this paper; then write the final answer for each problem on the smiley face next to its number.

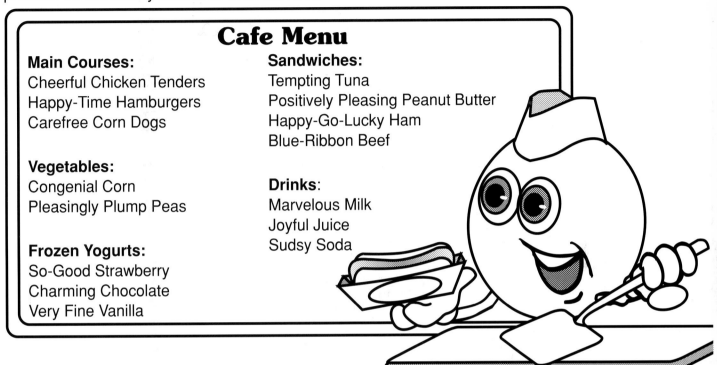

## Cafe Menu

**Main Courses:**
Cheerful Chicken Tenders
Happy-Time Hamburgers
Carefree Corn Dogs

**Vegetables:**
Congenial Corn
Pleasingly Plump Peas

**Frozen Yogurts:**
So-Good Strawberry
Charming Chocolate
Very Fine Vanilla

**Sandwiches:**
Tempting Tuna
Positively Pleasing Peanut Butter
Happy-Go-Lucky Ham
Blue-Ribbon Beef

**Drinks:**
Marvelous Milk
Joyful Juice
Sudsy Soda

 1. Harriet only wants one main course and one vegetable. How many possible combinations can she order?

 2. If Homer wants only one sandwich and one drink, how many possible combinations can he order?

 3. Harold is horribly hungry! He wants one main course, one vegetable, and one drink. How many possible combinations can he order?

 4. How many possible combinations can Henrietta order if she wants one, two, or three different flavors of yogurt?

 5. If Henrietta wants to add a fruit topping to her yogurt, how many more other choices does she have?

**Bonus Box:** Create a word problem for Mrs. Smiley on a separate sheet of paper. Give the problem to a friend to solve; then check to see that your friend does not repeat or leave out any items.

65

## How To Extend The Lesson:

- Instruct each student to create a list of his family's favorite breakfast foods. Suggest that he include main dishes such as cereal, eggs, and pancakes; side dishes such as toast, fruit, and bacon; and beverages such as juice, milk, or water. Have the student challenge a family member to list all the possible combinations for eating one main dish, one side dish, and one beverage *(27)*. Instruct the student to check the completed list for accuracy. If a choice has been repeated or omitted, direct the student to show the family member how to make an organized list of the choices. Finally, have each student write a paragraph about his experience and share it with the class.

- Have each student roll a die four times and record all the possible four-digit numbers that can be formed using those numbers *(up to 24 different numbers)*.

- Challenge each student to list all the possible combinations of outfits that can be made from two different kinds of shirts: a T-shirt and a tank top, two different kinds of outer covering: a sweatshirt and a parka, and two different kinds of pants: jeans and shorts *(8 different outfits)*.

- Have each student gather four classroom items—such as a pencil, an eraser, a piece of chalk, and a paper clip. Direct the student to challenge a classmate to list all the possible ways the four items can be arranged in left-to-right order. *(See the 24 different possible arrangements below.)* Instruct each student to check the completed list for accuracy.

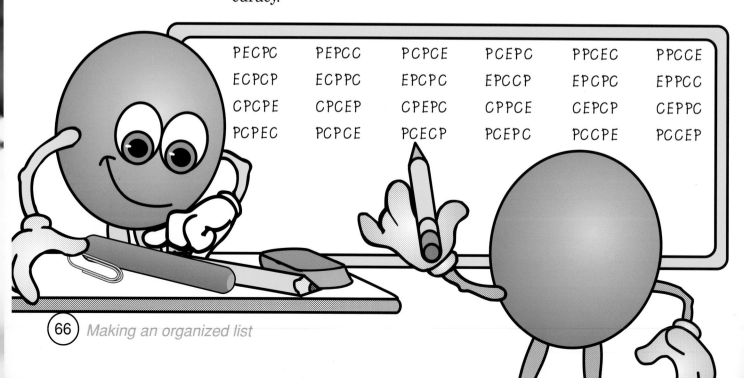

| | | | | | |
|---|---|---|---|---|---|
| PECPC | PEPCC | PCPCE | PCEPC | PPCEC | PPCCE |
| ECPCP | ECPPC | EPCPC | EPCCP | EPCPC | EPPCC |
| CPCPE | CPCEP | CPEPC | CPPCE | CEPCP | CEPPC |
| PCPEC | PCPCE | PCECP | PCEPC | PCCPE | PCCEP |

# Retrace Your Steps!

*Be super sleuthful and work backwards to solve problems.*

**Skill:** Working backwards to solve a problem

**Estimated Lesson Time:** 45 minutes

## Teacher Preparation:
1. Duplicate one copy of the reproducible on page 69 for each student.
2. Write the word problem from Step 1 on page 68 on a blank transparency.

## Materials:
1 copy of page 69 for each student
blank transparency
1 overhead marking pen

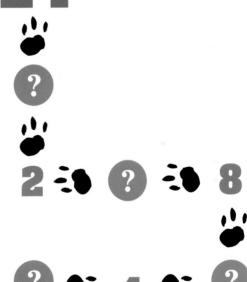

## Background Information:
Working backwards is a problem-solving strategy that involves making a series of computations, starting with data given at the end of the problem and ending with data presented at the beginning of the problem.

## PROBLEM-SOLVING STRATEGIES

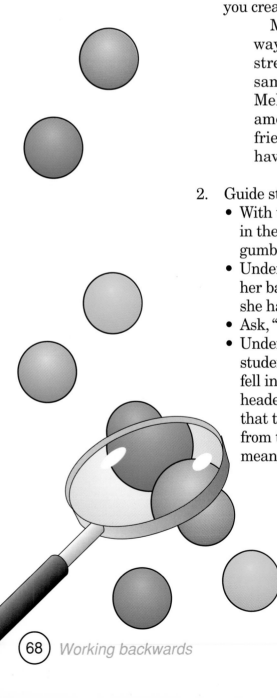

### Introducing The Lesson:

Begin by asking your students to recall different problem-solving strategies they have used. Possible answers could include *using logical reasoning, drawing a picture, acting it out or using objects, using or making a table, making an organized list, guessing and checking, using or looking for a pattern,* and *making it simpler*. Announce that today they will use a problem-solving strategy called *working backwards*.

### Steps:

1. Read the problem below to your class as you display the transparency you created.

    Melissa was carrying a bag of gumballs to school. On the way she dropped the bag and 20 gumballs rolled into the street drain. She stopped at the corner store and bought the same amount of gumballs that were left in her bag. When Melissa arrived at school, she divided all the gumballs equally among her 6 friends, keeping none for herself. Each of her friends received 11 gumballs. How many gumballs did she have in her bag when she left home?

2. Guide students through the steps below to solve this problem.
    - With the overhead marker, underline "11 gumballs" and "6 friends" in the problem above. Then ask, "If 6 friends each received 11 gumballs, how many gumballs did Melissa give away?" *(11 x 6 = 66)*
    - Underline "bought the same amount of gumballs that were left in her bag." Then ask, "If she bought the same amount of gumballs as she had after losing some, how many did she buy?" *(half of 66 = 33)*
    - Ask, "How many gumballs did not fall into the drain?" *(33)*
    - Underline "20 gumballs rolled into the street drain." Then help your students conclude that if Melissa had 33 gumballs plus the 20 that fell into the drain, then she must have had 53 gumballs as she headed to school. *(33 + 20 = 53)* Also help your students conclude that to solve the problem, they often had to use inverse operations from those suggested in the original problem (*divided equally* meant having to multiply to solve, etc.).

3. Change the problem above so that eight friends receive ten gumballs each. Have your students solve this new problem on their own to find out how many gumballs Melissa had before starting to school. *(60)*

4. Check your students' solutions to this problem; then distribute one copy of page 69 to each student. Direct each student to solve all six problems by working backwards.

Name _____

# Retrace Your Steps!

Have you ever misplaced something and then retraced your steps to try to find the missing item? This same method of problem solving can be used in math. Each problem below can be solved by using the strategy of working backwards. Solve each problem and write its solution in the space provided. *Kcul doog!* Oops, I mean good luck!

**1.**

Tia bought a hat for $10.95, and a sweatshirt that cost three times as much as the hat. She had $5.20 left. How much did she have before she bought the hat and sweatshirt?

_____

**2.**

Jacob's mom bought a huge bag of candy for him to share with his friends and his little brother, Ron. He gave 12 pieces to Ron, then divided the remaining pieces equally among himself and his three friends. Jacob ended up with 16 pieces of candy for himself. How many pieces of candy were in the bag that Jacob's mom bought?

_____

**3.**

Trina spent $12.70 of the money she had been saving in her piggy bank at the baseball game. She spent four times that amount the next day on a new radio for her bedroom. She only has $36.50 left. How much did Trina originally have in her piggy bank?

_____

**4.**

Antawn bought a box of baseball cards to start a collection. After two months of collecting, he had 20 more baseball cards. After six months of collecting, he had twice the cards he had after two months of collecting. Antawn had 90 baseball cards after six months of collecting. How many cards did Antawn have to start his collection?

_____

**5.**

Gabriella spent $12.00 on a shirt, $25.50 on jeans, and $7.35 for lunch while she was at the mall. She stopped at the music store and bought two CDs. Gabriella had $84.00 when she left the house and came home with $8.42 in her wallet. How much did she spend on CDs?

_____

**6.**

The number of students in Dominick's three-year-old school tripled for the start of the second school year. At the beginning of the third year, 30 new students joined. Dominick's school now has 210 students. How many students were enrolled in Dominick's school during the first year it was open?

_____

**Bonus Box:** On the back of this paper, write a problem similar to the ones above. Challenge a friend to solve your problem using the working-backwards strategy.

## How To Extend The Lesson:

- Reinforce the working-backwards problem-solving strategy with flowcharts. Have your students solve the problems below by using inverse operations—addition/subtraction or multiplication/division. Once your students become successful with solving this type of problem, challenge them to create flowcharts of their own. Have each student write each flowchart that he creates on an index card. Post all the index cards on a bulletin board titled "Reverse Your Thinking" that students can visit during their free time.

$\bigcirc + 3 = \triangle \times 4 = \square - 4 = \bigcirc \div 2 = 20$ (*solution: 8, 11, 44, 40*)

$\triangle \times 2 = \square + 6 = \bigcirc \div 3 = \triangle + 4 = 10$ (*solution: 6, 12, 18, 6*)

$\square \times 3 = \triangle - 10 = \bigcirc \div 2 = 13$ (*solution: 12, 36, 26*)

$\bigcirc + 7 = \square \times 4 = \triangle \times 3 = \bigcirc \div 5 = 36$ (*solution: 8, 15, 60, 180*)

- Play a mind-reading game with your students to practice the working-backwards problem-solving strategy. Create a variety of problems similar to the one shown below. Write each problem on the board one at a time. Read each problem aloud to your students. Then direct them to work backwards through the information in the problem to read your mind and determine the mystery number. After a few rounds of this game, challenge each student to come up with a problem for a classmate to solve.

- I am thinking of a number. If you multiply my number by 2, add 4, subtract 6, and then divide by 2, the result is 14. What is my number?

  Solution: The number is 15.
  $14 \times 2 = 28 + 6 = 34 - 4 = 30 \div 2 = 15$

# On A Roll!

*Set and win high stakes with this fun graphing lesson!*

**Skills:** Collecting and recording data; making a bar graph

**Estimated Lesson Time:** 45 minutes

**Teacher Preparation:**
Duplicate one copy of page 73 for each student.

**Materials:**
colored chalk—red, blue, green, yellow, and orange
1 copy of page 73 for each student
scissors
several pieces of clear tape for each student
crayons or colored pencils

**Background Information:**
A *graph* is a drawing that shows and compares data. *Data* is any set of information that can be collected and tallied. Some different kinds of graphs are listed below.

- *Bar graph*—a graph that shows information with bars of different lengths
- *Circle graph*—a graph that shows how a whole is divided into parts
- *Line graph*—a graph that shows changes in data over a period of time
- *Pictograph*—a graph that shows numerical information with pictures

## Introducing The Lesson:

Begin by showing your students how handy a bar graph can be. Quickly ask each student in turn to name his favorite ice-cream flavor. Next ask a student if he remembers how many of his classmates selected vanilla as their favorite flavor. Expect this child to have difficulty remembering. Do the same thing for the flavors of chocolate, strawberry, cookie dough, and mint chocolate chip. Then help your students conclude that there must be an easy way to record and access information of this type.

## Steps:

1. Explain that graphs are one way to represent collected data. Ask your students to name several places where graphs can be seen. (*newspapers, magazines, posters, television, etc.*)

2. Explain that you will construct a bar graph that shows the favorite colors of the class.

3. Write the following words as headings on the left side of your chalkboard: "red," "blue," "green," "yellow," and "orange." Direct each student to silently select one of these choices as his favorite color.

4. Call the name of each color choice one at a time. As you do, direct each student to raise his hand when you call his favorite color. Record a tally mark beside the appropriate heading for each child who raises his hand.

5. On the right side of your board, draw a grid that has five vertical columns of squares equal to the largest number of recorded tally marks. Title this grid "Our Favorite Colors." Label the horizontal axis with the names of the five colors; then label the vertical axis with appropriate numerical increments. Afterward color each bar on the graph to represent the number of tally marks recorded for that color.

6. Give each student a pair of scissors, several pieces of clear tape, crayons or colored pencils, and a copy of page 73. Instruct him to complete the sheet according to its directions to create a bar graph of his own.

Name________________________________________ *Making a bar graph*

# You're On A Roll!

**Directions:** Cut out the cube pattern at the bottom of this sheet; then fold and tape the pattern along its sides to make a die. Roll the die 20 times, recording the result of each roll in the tally chart below. Then color the bar graph below the tally chart to show your results.

Tally Chart

| ○ | △ | □ | ☆ | ◠ | ⏢ |
|---|---|---|---|---|---|
| | | | | | |

Bar Graph

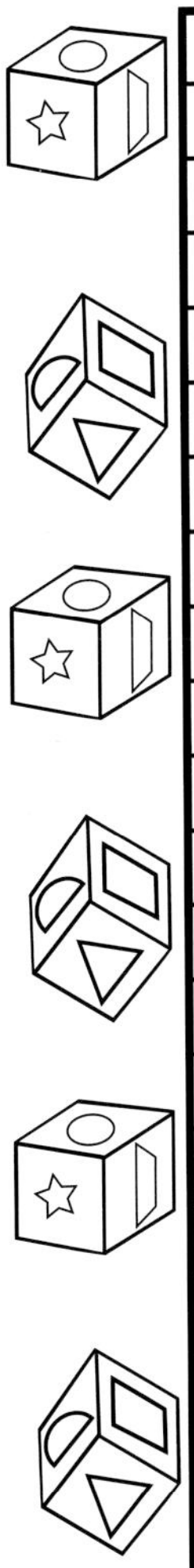

| | | | | | | |
|---|---|---|---|---|---|---|
| 20 | | | | | | |
| 19 | | | | | | |
| 18 | | | | | | |
| 17 | | | | | | |
| 16 | | | | | | |
| 15 | | | | | | |
| 14 | | | | | | |
| 13 | | | | | | |
| 12 | | | | | | |
| 11 | | | | | | |
| 10 | | | | | | |
| 9 | | | | | | |
| 8 | | | | | | |
| 7 | | | | | | |
| 6 | | | | | | |
| 5 | | | | | | |
| 4 | | | | | | |
| 3 | | | | | | |
| 2 | | | | | | |
| 1 | | | | | | |
| | ○ | △ | □ | ☆ | ◠ | ⏢ |

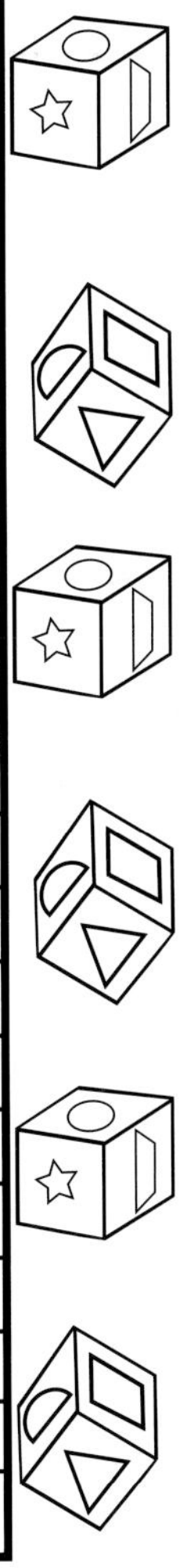

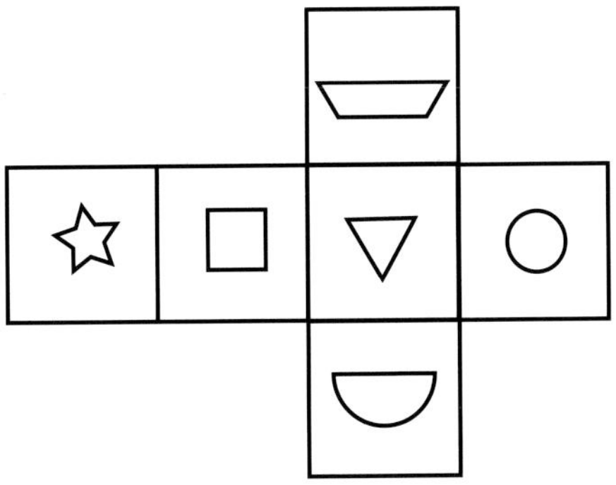

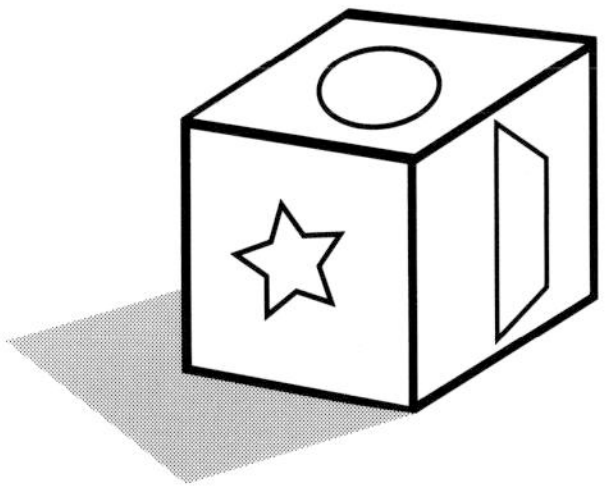

**GRAPHING, PROBABILITY, & STATISTICS**

## How To Extend The Lesson:

- Have your students represent the data collected for this lesson in a different kind of graph—such as a line graph, a pictograph, or a circle graph.

- As a class, brainstorm the titles of favorite movies. Afterward write your students' responses on sentence strips and display them along one wall of your classroom. Then have your students form a people graph by directing each student to stand in a line in front of the sentence strip that names her favorite movie. Instruct the first person in each line to count the number of students in her line and in turn report this total aloud. Record each total on the chalkboard under an appropriate heading. Then ask your students several questions similar to those in extension three below.

- Review Venn diagrams with your students. Afterward draw two large, overlapping hoops on poster board. Display the hoops in the center of a small bulletin board. With a marker, write the word "Chocolate" above the left-hand hoop, "Vanilla" above the right-hand hoop, and "Twist" above the shared section. Above the hoops, write "Which Is Your Favorite Flavor Of Ice Cream?" Allow each student to come up during free time and indicate his preference of flavors by making a tally mark inside the appropriate hoop. When all students have marked their preferences, ask questions like the following: "How many students responded to the question?", "Which is the most popular flavor?", and "How many more/fewer students prefer twist than vanilla or chocolate?"

# What Are The Chances?

*Chances are your students will find
this probability lesson absolutely "ribbit-ing"!*

**Skill:** Exploring probable outcomes and determining probability

**Estimated Lesson Time:** 30 minutes

## Teacher Preparation:

1. Cut a sheet of drawing paper in half vertically and write "FAMILY" in capital letters across one half of the paper. On the other half of the paper, write "CLASSROOM."
2. Duplicate one copy of page 77 for each student.

## Materials:

1 copy of page 77 for each student
1 sheet of drawing paper
1 paper bag
scissors
marker

I had a one-in-six chance of rolling the five.

## Background Information:

• *Probability* is the measure of the likelihood of an event.
• A *probable outcome* is what is likely to happen in that event based on its probability.

## Introducing The Lesson:

Introduce this lesson by showing students the word "FAMILY" on the drawing paper. While students are watching, cut off one letter at a time from the word and place it in the paper bag.

## Steps:

1. Ask your students the following series of questions:
   - How many pieces of paper are in the bag? *(six)*
   - How many pieces of paper have a different letter written on them? *(six)*
   - If I reach into the bag and pull out one paper, what are the chances of it being the F? A? M? I? L? Y? *(The chances of drawing each letter are one out of six, or 1/6.)*
   - Does each letter have an equal chance of being drawn? *(yes)*
   - What are the chances of drawing the letter S? *(0/6; impossible)*

2. Empty the bag and repeat the procedure in "Introducing The Lesson" with the word "CLASSROOM." Then ask the following questions:
   - How many pieces of paper are in the bag? *(nine)*
   - How many pieces of paper have a different letter on them? *(seven)*
   - If I reach into the bag and pull out one paper, what are the chances of it being the C? L? A? S? R? O? M? *(The probability of drawing a C, an L, an A, an R, or an M is 1/9. The probability of drawing an O or an S is 2/9.)*
   - Does each letter have an equal chance of being drawn? *(no)*
   - What are the chances of drawing a Y? *(0/9; impossible)*

3. Instruct each student to determine the probability of drawing each letter in his first and last name from a bag.

4. Give each student a copy of page 77 and have him complete the page as directed on the reproducible.

Name _____

# What Are The Chances?

Here is your chance to show what you know about probable outcomes! Read the ten problems below and determine the probability of each one. Write your answers in fraction form on the lines provided. Be sure to express each probability in fraction form.

1. Each side of this cube has a different color written on it. What is the probability of rolling green?

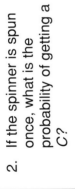

_____

2. If the spinner is spun once, what is the probability of getting a C?

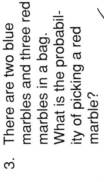

_____

3. There are two blue marbles and three red marbles in a bag. What is the probability of picking a red marble?

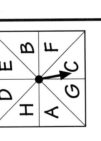

_____

4. What is the probability of a coin landing on heads, if you flip it once?

_____

5. What is the probability of rolling an even number with a single die?

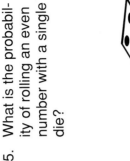

_____

6. Adam tossed a coin six times and got heads each time. What is the probability that he will get heads on the seventh toss?

_____

7. Katlyn has four pennies, two nickels, a dime, and three quarters in her pocket. If she takes out one coin, what is the probability that it will be a nickel?

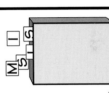

_____

8. If each letter in the word "MISSISSIPPI" is cut out and placed in a bag, what is the probability of pulling out the letter I?

_____

9. C. J. has 15 baseball cards. Eight cards show a right-handed batter, and seven cards show a left-handed batter. If he picks one card, what is the probability that the card will show a left-handed batter?

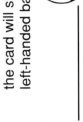

_____

10. What is the probability of spinning a T?

_____

**Bonus Box:** On the back of this page, design a spinner. Then write a probability question that can be answered using the spinner, and challenge a friend to answer it.

©1997 The Education Center, Inc. • *Lifesaver Lessons*™ • Grade 4 • TEC506 • Key p. 96

## How To Extend The Lesson:

- Divide your class into pairs. Give each pair one die. Instruct each pair to roll the die 30 times and record the results of each roll. Then have the pair analyze its data to see if the results are consistent with the probability of this event.

- Give each group of students a paper bag filled with one red crayon, one yellow crayon, and one blue crayon. Direct each group to, without looking, pull one crayon from the bag 20 different times and record the results. Then have each group compare its results with those from other groups.

- Divide your class into pairs. Give each pair a copy of the blank spinner below, a brad, and a paper clip. Instruct the pair to create a game using the spinner (see the example below). Then allow the pair to try out its game on the class. Have the class decide which spinner games are fair and which are not.

Spin the spinner three times and total the results. If the sum of all three numbers is less than eight, you win a sticker.

# On Your Mark, Get Set, Go!

*Your students will be in for a fantastic finish with this quick and easy lesson on adding and subtracting decimals!*

**Skill:** Adding and subtracting decimal numbers to the hundredths place

**Estimated Lesson Time:** 1 hour

## Teacher Preparation:
1. Write the steps and examples for adding and subtracting decimal numbers shown below on a sheet of chart paper.
2. Duplicate one copy of page 81 for each group of four students.

## Materials:
1 sheet of chart paper
1 marker
For each group of four students:
- 1 stopwatch or a watch with a second hand
- 1 sheet of loose-leaf paper and a pencil
- 1 copy of page 81
- 1 die
For each student:
- 1 pair of scissors
- 1 crayon
- 1 sheet of loose-leaf paper and a pencil

## Background Information:
To add and subtract decimals, first line up the decimal points; then add and subtract as with whole numbers. Annex zeros to form equivalent decimals and hold places wherever necessary. Position the decimal point in the resulting sum or difference.

### Adding And Subtracting Decimals

**Step 1:**
Line up the decimal points. Add zeros to form equivalent decimals if necessary.
**Examples:**

```
  1.60          1.60
+ 0.85        – 0.85
```

**Step 2:**
Add/subtract the hundredths; then add/subtract the tenths. Regroup if necessary.
**Examples:**

```
   1                0 15 10
  1.60             1̸.6̸0̸
+ 0.85            – 0.8 5
   45                75
```

**Step 3:**
Add/subtract the ones. Regroup if necessary. Write the decimal point.
**Examples:**

```
   1                0 15 10
  1.60             1̸.6̸0̸
+ 0.85            – 0.8 5
  2.45              0.75
```

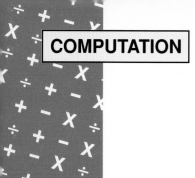

## Introducing The Lesson:

Have four student volunteers come to the front of the classroom. Pair these students; then give each pair a stopwatch. Direct one student in the pair to be the timer and the other to be the participant. On your signal, direct the participant to do 25 jumping jacks, 25 toe touches, and 25 knee bends while the timer uses the watch to determine how many minutes and seconds it takes the participant to do all three exercises. After each participant has finished, have each timer record the time on the chalkboard. Next ask students, "How can we find the total time it took to do the exercises?" and "How can we find the difference between the two times?" *(add the two times together; subtract the shorter time from the longer time)* Compute the total for and the difference in these times on the chalkboard, explaining that—after aligning decimal points—adding and subtracting decimal numbers is just like adding and subtracting whole numbers.

## Steps:

1. Refer to the chart you programmed earlier with the steps and examples from page 79 to explain how to add and subtract two decimal numbers.

2. Next divide your students into groups of four. Supply each group with a stopwatch, a sheet of loose-leaf paper, and a pencil.

3. Direct each group to determine four activities it would like to time—such as hopping on one foot 25 times, reciting the alphabet three times, counting to 100, or writing "School is cool!" ten times. Have each group prepare a chart on its paper, listing each activity and each group member's name as shown in the example.

4. Have the members of each group take turns timing one another to find out how long it takes to complete each activity and record the times on the team chart.

5. After timing each member for every activity, direct each group to first calculate the total of and then the difference in the two highest times, the two middle times, and the highest and lowest times. Call on volunteers to share examples in which zeros were annexed to help with the adding and subtracting.

6. Distribute one die and a copy of page 81 to each group. Instruct each group to follow the directions on the sheet to complete the activity.

*Adding and subtracting decimals*

# The Decimal 500

In auto racing, a driver can win or lose by just one hundredth of a second—so every second counts! Get in on the race at the *Decimal 500* and go for a fantastic finish!

**Directions:** Cut out the track, race cars, and lap cards. Give a different race car to each player to color. Put the lap cards in the center of the track. Place each car on the *Start* block. Each player, in turn, should roll a die, move the correct number of spaces, and then add or subtract the time as directed on that gameboard space. Do all calculations on loose-leaf paper. Each time a player completes a lap, he or she should take a lap card. The player with the lowest total time after five laps is the winner.

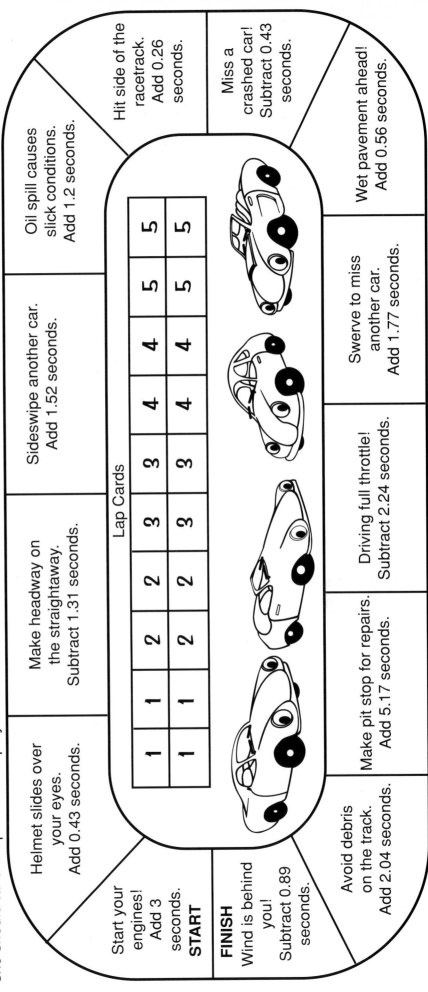

Hit side of the racetrack. Add 0.26 seconds.

Miss a crashed car! Subtract 0.43 seconds.

Oil spill causes slick conditions. Add 1.2 seconds.

Wet pavement ahead! Add 0.56 seconds.

Sideswipe another car. Add 1.52 seconds.

Swerve to miss another car. Add 1.77 seconds.

Make headway on the straightaway. Subtract 1.31 seconds.

Lap Cards

| 1 | 2 | 3 | 4 | 5 |
|---|---|---|---|---|
| 1 | 2 | 3 | 4 | 5 |

Driving full throttle! Subtract 2.24 seconds.

Helmet slides over your eyes. Add 0.43 seconds.

Make pit stop for repairs. Add 5.17 seconds.

Start your engines! Add 3 seconds. **START**

**FINISH** Wind is behind you! Subtract 0.89 seconds.

Avoid debris on the track. Add 2.04 seconds.

**Note To The Teacher:** Provide each student with scissors, a different-colored crayon or marker, a sheet of loose-leaf paper, and a pencil. After the group completes each round, have the players check one another's answers for accuracy.

## How To Extend The Lesson:

• Gather a selection of advertisement pages from a newspaper. Then, using the ads, create product coupons for 10 to 20 of the items listed. Place the coupons and the ads at a center. Direct your students to use the center one at a time. Have each student choose six different coupons and find the prices of these six products in the ad pages. Next have the student add or subtract the appropriate amounts to find the price of each product after deducting its coupon amount, the total coupon savings, and the total amount of the purchase before and after using the coupons.

• Have each student search through any section of the newspaper for four decimal numbers—such as precipitation amounts, timed sporting events, and stock-exchange values. Direct each student to use those four numbers to first determine the totals of and then the differences in the two highest numbers, the two middle numbers, and the highest and lowest numbers.

• Gather an index card for each student in your class. On half of the cards, write an addition or a subtraction equation. On the remaining cards, write the solutions to the equation cards. Shuffle the cards; then have each student choose a different card. Direct each student with an equation card to solve the equation, and then search for the classmate who has the solution card for that equation. Finally, instruct the student with the solution card to check the worked equation for accuracy. Collect and shuffle the cards; then repeat the process as long as time permits.

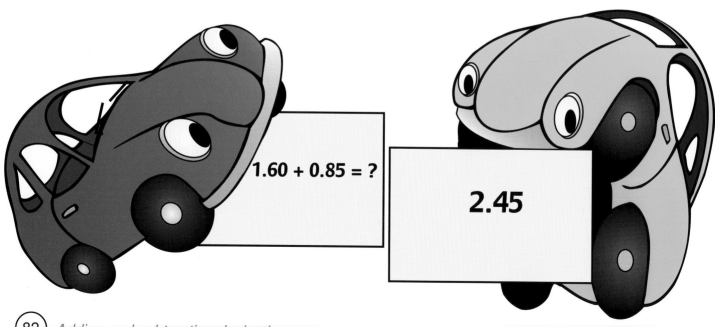

$$1.60 + 0.85 = ?$$

$$2.45$$

# Focusing On Fractions

*Zero in on adding and subtracting fractions with like denominators.*

**Skill:** Adding and subtracting like fractions; reducing fractions to simplest terms

**Estimated Lesson Time:** 1 hour

## Teacher Preparation:

1. Use a ruler to divide a sheet of 8 1/2" x 11" paper into 11 equal strips. Leaving the first strip whole, divide and label each of the remaining ten strips into halves, thirds, fourths, fifths, sixths, sevenths, eighths, ninths, tenths, and twelfths in that order as shown on page 84.
2. Duplicate two copies of this fraction-strip sheet for each student.
3. Duplicate one copy of page 85 for each student.

## Materials:

2 copies of the fraction-strip sheet
  for each student
a pair of scissors for each student
crayons
1 copy of page 85 for each student
1 sheet of 8 1/2" x 11" white paper
1 colored marker

## Background Information:

Adding and subtracting fractions with like denominators can involve renaming fractions as well as reducing them to lowest terms. To add or subtract fractions with like denominators, first add (or subtract) the numerators. Next write the sum (or difference) over the common denominator. Then write the resulting fraction in its simplest form by reducing or renaming it. For example, to add 6/12 and 3/12, add 6 and 3 to get a numerator of 9. Next write 9 over the common denominator of 12 to make the fraction 9/12. Then reduce 9/12 to its lowest terms of 3/4.

$$\frac{6}{12} + \frac{3}{12} = \frac{9}{12} = \frac{3}{4}$$

Steps:
1. Note that the denominators are the same.
2. Add the numerators 6 and 3 to get 9/12.
3. Reduce 9/12 to get 3/4.

## Introducing The Lesson:

Begin by folding a sheet of white paper into fourths; then color one section of the paper with a marker. Ask your students to name the part of the paper that you colored as a fraction *(1/4)*. Next color another section of the paper. Then ask your students to identify this new fraction *(2/4)*. Ask them to find another name for this fraction *(1/2)*. Afterward write "1/4 + 1/4 = 2/4 = 1/2" on your chalkboard to record this process as an equation.

## Steps:

1.  Give each student two copies of the fraction-strip sheets, scissors, and crayons. Have him color each fraction strip on one of his sheets a different color. Then direct him to color his second sheet exactly like the first. Afterward instruct him to cut one of his sheets into strips of fraction pieces and to leave his second sheet uncut for use as a work mat.

2.  Have your students work along with you as you model how to use these manipulatives to show 1/4 + 1/4 = 2/4 = 1/2. First place two pieces labeled 1/4 on a work mat so that they cover two of the sections labeled fourths. Then lift these pieces and use them to cover the section labeled one-half. Help your students conclude that this model shows the equation written on the board.

3.  Write the addition problems below on your chalkboard. Direct each student to use his fraction-strip pieces to help him find each problem's sum and record it on loose-leaf paper.
    2/5 + 2/5 = 4/5
    2/6 + 3/6 = 5/6
    4/9 + 5/9 = 9/9 or 1
    5/10 + 2/10 = 7/10
    6/12 + 3/12 = 9/12 = 3/4

4.  Ask your students if they can identify a pattern associated with adding fractions that have the same denominators. *(The numerators are added, but not the denominators. The denominator stays the same.)*

5.  Review the steps for adding and subtracting like fractions (see page 83). Afterward have each student show these steps on paper for each problem he worked in Step 3 above.

6.  Give each student a copy of page 85 to complete as directed.

# It's In The Bag!

Read the riddle below. To solve this riddle, just work the problems on this sheet on loose-leaf paper. (Hint: If you solve a problem correctly, you'll find its answer written on one of the cans pictured on the grocery bag below.) Write each answer and corresponding letter in the blanks next to each problem. Then match each answer's letter to its corresponding problem number at the bottom of this sheet to solve the riddle.

**Riddle:** What might a feline say when she has given away a secret?

|  | Problem | Answer | Corresponding letter |
|---|---|---|---|
| 1. | $5/12 + 2/12 =$ | _____ | = _____ |
| 2. | $13/14 - 3/14 =$ | _____ | = _____ |
| 3. | $7/15 + 3/15 =$ | _____ | = _____ |
| 4. | $13/16 - 9/16 =$ | _____ | = _____ |
| 5. | $4/10 + 1/10 =$ | _____ | = _____ |
| 6. | $8/9 - 1/9 =$ | _____ | = _____ |
| 7. | $3/18 + 7/18 =$ | _____ | = _____ |
| 8. | $1/6 + 1/6 =$ | _____ | = _____ |
| 9. | $20/21 - 17/21 =$ | _____ | = _____ |
| 10. | $9/16 + 5/16 =$ | _____ | = _____ |
| 11. | $5/15 - 2/15 =$ | _____ | = _____ |
| 12. | $7/16 - 5/16 =$ | _____ | = _____ |
| 13. | $2/7 + 5/7 =$ | _____ | = _____ |
| 14. | $11/12 - 1/12 =$ | _____ | = _____ |
| 15. | $7/10 + 1/10 =$ | _____ | = _____ |
| 16. | $9/11 - 2/11 =$ | _____ | = _____ |
| 17. | $1/9 + 3/9 =$ | _____ | = _____ |
| 18. | $17/25 - 7/25 =$ | _____ | = _____ |
| 19. | $1/8 + 5/8 =$ | _____ | = _____ |
| 20. | $19/20 - 1/20 =$ | _____ | = _____ |

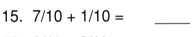

**Answer:** ___ ___ ___   ___ ___ ___   ___ ___   ___ ___ ___
   2  19  7    12  4  10    15  17    11  1  8

___ ___ ___   ___ ___ ___   ___ ___ ___ ___
 9   3        13  16  20     18  6  14  5

## How To Extend The Lesson:

I have 2/4!

2/4

That reduces to 1/2!

1/2

That's equivalent to 4/8!

4/8

- Gather 21 index cards to make a center game. On ten of these cards, write problems that involve addition or subtraction of like fractions. On the other ten cards, write the answers for these problems. Use the extra card for an answer key. Next shuffle each set of ten cards and spread them facedown on a table at a center along with paper and pencils. Allow two students at a time to use this center. Direct one student to turn over two cards, one from the problem-card deck and one from the answer-card deck. Have this student solve her problem on paper. If she solves the problem and the answer card she turned over is a match, instruct her to keep both cards. If she does not solve the problem correctly or if the answer card is not a match, direct her to put the cards back in their original places on the table. Then have the other partner take her turn. After all the cards have been claimed, have each partner count her cards. The winner is the student with the most cards.

- Cut out action pictures from different magazines. Group your students in threes; then give each group a picture, glue, and a sheet of 9" x 12" paper. Direct each group to create a word problem that uses the information presented in its picture. Explain that each problem must involve adding or subtracting like fractions. Have each group glue its picture to the top of its paper, write its problem at the bottom, and record the answer on the back. Collect all the papers; then distribute a different paper to each group. Direct each group to solve the problem on its paper without peeking at the answer.

- Write sets of related fractions on different index cards, one fraction on each card. Afterward place these cards inside a bag and have each student draw out one card. Instruct each student in turn to hold up his card and share his fraction aloud. As he does, direct the other students to tell whether their fractions are related to his fraction in some way—perhaps an equivalent or reduced form. For example, if the fraction 2/4 is announced, students with the cards 4/8 (an equivalent fraction) and 1/2 (a reduced equivalent fraction) could identify that they have related fractions. Continue in this manner until every student has shared his card.

# Monkeying Around With Mental Math

*Your students will go bananas over this mental-math game!*

**Skill:** Using mental math to solve basic computation

**Estimated Lesson Time:** 45 minutes

$$8 \times 6 + 10 - 8 =$$

## Teacher Preparation:

1. Duplicate one copy of page 89 for each pair of students.
2. Duplicate the answer key for page 89 found on page 96.
3. Duplicate one copy of the directions on page 88 for each pair, or make a transparency of the directions.

## Materials:

1 copy of page 89 for each pair of students
1 copy of the answer key on page 96
1 pair of scissors for each pair of students
1 copy of the directions on page 88 for each pair
   of students (or a transparency of the directions)

## Background Information:

Mental math can either involve finding the exact answer to a problem *(mental computation)* or only an approximate answer to a problem *(estimation)*.

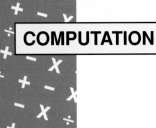

## Introducing The Lesson:

Introduce this lesson by asking, "About how many hours do you spend at school each day?" Allow a few students to respond; then point out that this question asks for an estimate. Next ask, "How many hours are between 1:00 P.M. and 3:00 P.M.?" *(two)* Point out that the second question required an exact answer.

## Steps:

1. Explain that sometimes math is done without a pencil and paper or a calculator. Point out that a pencil or calculator was not needed to answer the two questions above. Share the background information on page 87 with your students.

2. Ask students to name everyday situations in which mental math can be used. List all responses on the chalkboard.

3. Have students decide which of the situations listed on the board might require an exact answer instead of an estimate.

4. Tell students that mental math is used every day and that their mental computation skills can improve with practice.

5. Pair your students and distribute one copy of page 89, one copy of the directions at the bottom of this page (or display the transparency, if you created one), and one pair of scissors to each pair.

6. Instruct the pair to play the game as directed. While the pairs play, post the answer key on the chalkboard for students to use when checking their work.

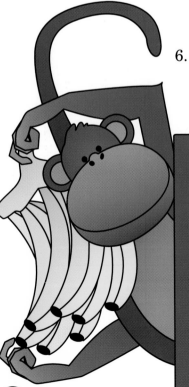

### Directions For Mental-Math Game

**Set up:**
1. Cut apart each card and place it facedown in a shuffled pile.
2. Number a sheet of loose-leaf paper from 1 to 25.

To play:
1. Each player, in turn, flips over the top card. Players A and B each solve the problem on the card and write an answer next to the number on their paper that matches the card number.
2. The first player to write his answer circles that problem's number.
3. Continue play until each problem is solved.
4. Check your answers with the answer key that your teacher posted. Each player receives one point for every correct answer and two points for every circled correct answer. The player with the most points is the winner.

**5** first three multiples of 6

**10** $10.5 + 12 =$

**15** value of 1 quarter, 3 dimes, 2 nickels, and 3 pennies

**20** $60 \div 10 + 24 - 5 =$

**25** number of hours between 11:00 A.M. and 2:30 P.M.

**4** value of 2 quarters, 4 dimes, and 6 pennies

**9** area of a 5 x 9 rectangle

**14** number of sides on 4 pentagons

**19** first four multiples of 8

**24** $45 \div 5 - 5 + 12 =$

**3** number of inches in 4 feet

**8** number of angles in 6 triangles

**13** $77 - 7 + 12 =$

**18** 45,890 rounded to the nearest hundred

**23** number of days in the months of May, June, and July

**2** $4 \times 7 \div 2 + 10 =$

**7** number of days in 5 weeks minus the number of minutes in one half hour

**12** number of hours between 12:30 P.M. and 5:00 P.M.

**17** change received from a $20.00 bill after spending $12.45

**22** value of 3 quarters, 3 dimes, and 4 pennies

**1** number of days in 8 weeks

**6** $3 \times 9 + 5 - 4 =$

**11** $40,000 \div 40 =$

**16** number of minutes in 3 hours

**21** perimeter of a 3 x 4 rectangle

**Note To The Teacher:** Duplicate one copy for each pair of students.

## How To Extend The Lesson:

• When assigning a page of basic computation for your students to complete, instruct them to first use mental math to come up with an estimated answer for each problem. Emphasize to students the importance of using estimation as a tool for checking to see if their answers are appropriate.

• Divide your class into pairs. Give each pair a sales flyer or catalog and a calculator. Instruct one student to be the cashier and the other the customer. Have the customer choose one item to purchase and pretend to give the cashier a larger amount of cash. For example, if an item costs $5.65, give a 10- or 20-dollar bill. Direct the cashier to mentally calculate the correct amount of change that's due. Then have the pair use a calculator to check. Give one point to the cashier for a correct answer. Instruct the pair to switch roles and repeat the process. When time expires, declare the student with the most points the winner.

• Start having Mental-Math Mondays in your classroom! Each Monday read aloud a series of ten mental-math problems for your students to solve. Have each student record and check her answers in the same notebook each week. After about five weeks, show students how to create a graph to track their mental-math progress.

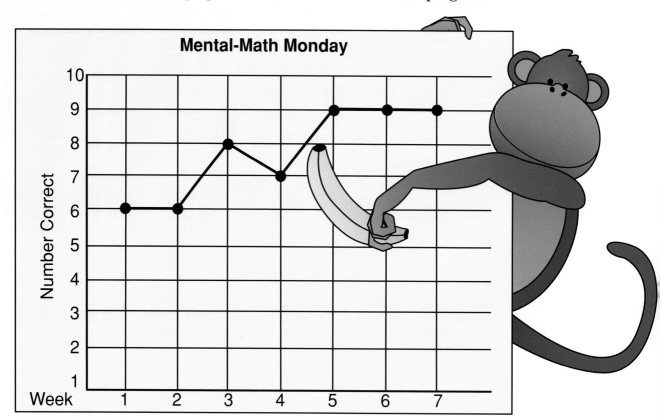

# Adventures In Averaging

*Here's the easy, step-by-step lesson on finding averages that you've "bean" looking for!*

**Skill:** Finding the average—or mean—of a set of numbers

**Estimated Lesson Time:** 45 minutes

## Teacher Preparation:
1. Duplicate one copy of page 93 for each student.
2. Fill three plastic cups, each with a different number of jelly beans (or different-colored plastic chips)—10 beans in the first cup, 12 beans in the second cup, and 8 beans in the third cup.

## Materials:
1 copy of page 93 for each child
1 bag of jelly beans
   (or different-colored
   plastic chips)
5 clear plastic cups

## Background Information:
The numerical average of a set of numbers is called the *mean*. To find the mean, divide the sum of a set of numbers by the number of its addends.

## Introducing The Lesson:

Place the three cups of jelly beans (or colored chips) on a table in the front of your classroom. Have three student volunteers come forward and, in turn, empty one of the three plastic cups onto the table, counting the number of beans poured from the cup. Record the three totals on the board in a column as an addition problem. Explain to your class that the average—or mean—of the beans is found by adding the three totals together and dividing the sum by the number of cups into which the beans were divided. Demonstrate this process for your students.

## Steps:

1. Point out that the divisor used to find an average, or mean, is equal to the total number of addends used. Explain that if four cups had been used, the divisor would have been four instead of three.

2. Then explain that the average can be checked by combining the contents of the three cups together, and then sorting the jelly beans into three equal groups. Point out that if the average is computed correctly, it should equal the number of beans in each group. Test this by having a different student volunteer combine the three piles of beans and divide them evenly into three groups. Ask the student to compare the mean previously computed with the number of beans in each group.

3. Repeat this averaging exercise by varying the number of cups and the number of beans in each cup. In order to avoid a fractional mean, be sure that the total number of beans used is evenly divisible by the number of cups used. For example, if 32 beans are randomly placed into five cups, the average number of beans per cup—or mean—would be six and two-fifths. But if 30 beans are used, the mean would be six.

4. Give each student one copy of page 93 for additional practice.

# Just What You've "Bean" Looking For!

The students in Mrs. Lundein's class earn jelly beans for good behavior. The chart below shows how jelly beans were distributed over the past week in her class. Use the chart to fill in the missing information.

The *average* of a set of numbers is called the *mean*. To find the mean, divide the sum of a set of numbers by the number of its addends. For example, the average number of jelly beans Mrs. Lundein gave out to each student on Monday can be determined by completing the following steps:

**Step 1**  Find the sum of the numbers to be averaged. *5 + 9 + 6 + 7 + 10 + 5 = 42*
**Step 2**  Divide the sum by the number of addends.  *42 ÷ 6 = 7*

| | M | T | W | T | F | Weekly Total | Average |
|---|---|---|---|---|---|---|---|
| Nicholas | 5 | 7 | 5 | 5 | 8 | | |
| Angela | 9 | 8 | 4 | 6 | 3 | | |
| Alexander | 6 | 4 | 8 | 5 | 2 | | |
| Gregory | 7 | 5 | 10 | 4 | 4 | | |
| Sarah | 10 | 4 | 6 | 7 | 3 | | |
| Jackie | 5 | 8 | 9 | 9 | 4 | | |
| **Daily Total** | | | | | | | |
| **Average** | | | | | | | |

**Directions:** Use the completed chart to answer the following questions.

1. On the average, who received the most jelly beans per day for the week?

   _____

2. Was the average number of jelly beans given out by Mrs. Lundein higher on Monday or Friday?

   _____

3. Was the average number of jelly beans given to Sarah for the week higher or lower than the average number given to Alexander? _____

4. On which day did Mrs. Lundein give out the lowest average number of jelly beans?

   _____

**Bonus Box:** On the back of this sheet, write three additional problems of your own relating to the table above. Then exchange papers with a classmate and solve one another's problems.

©1997 The Education Center, Inc. • *Lifesaver Lessons*™ • Grade 4 • TEC506 • Key p. 96

## How To Extend The Lesson:

- Challenge your students to gather data from an almanac to write several word problems involving the computation of averages. Have the students exchange their problems with one another and complete them for additional practice.

- Extend your study of averages into social studies by having your students find the average population of different geographic regions of the United States. Graph the resulting averages to determine which regions are the most heavily populated.

- Collect a weather report featuring the high and low temperatures in your area from a local newspaper. Have your students use the data in that report to compute the average high and low temperatures for the week. Be sure to have students round the temperatures to the nearest whole number.

### This Week's Weather In Review

|          | High | Low |
|----------|------|-----|
| Monday   | 78   | 56  |
| Tuesday  | 80   | 61  |
| Wednesday| 74   | 45  |
| Thursday | 72   | 44  |
| Friday   | 73   | 46  |
| Saturday | 76   | 55  |
| Sunday   | 81   | 57  |

Average High Temperature:
78 + 80 + 74 + 72 + 73 + 76 + 81 = 534

534 ÷ 7 = 76.28 degrees
(rounds to 76 degrees)

Average Low Temperature:
56 + 61 + 45 + 44 + 46 + 55 + 57 = 364

364 ÷ 7 = 52 degrees

# Answer Key

## Page 9
1. 1,200
2. 2,200
3. 1,400
4. 1,700
5. 1,600
6. 900
7. 1,800
8. 1,000
9. 500
10. 1,700
11. 1,100
12. 1,800
13. 1,400
14. 1,400
15. 900
16. 1,300

## Page 13
1. All of the numbers have an 8 in the hundreds place.
2. 1,046 ft. < 1,050 ft. < 1,136 ft. < 1,250 ft. < 1,368 ft. < 1,454 ft.
3. Answers will vary. Possible answers include:

| | |
|---|---|
| 143,244 > 31,700 | 31,700 < 143,244 |
| 143,244 > 26,828 | 26,828 < 31,700 |
| 143,244 > 22,300 | 26,828 < 143,244 |
| 143,244 > 11,150 | 22,300 < 31,700 |
| 31,700 > 22,300 | 22,300 < 143,244 |
| 31,700 > 26,828 | 22,300 < 26,828 |
| 31,700 > 11,150 | 11,150 < 143,244 |
| 26,828 > 22,300 | 11,150 < 31,700 |
| 26,828 > 11,150 | 11,150 < 26,828 |
| 22,300 > 11,150 | 11,150 < 22,300 |

4. 29,028 ft. > 20,320 ft. > 19,340 ft. > 16,864 ft. > 16,500 ft.
5. 13,000 ft. < 13,350 ft. < 13,400 ft. < 13,680 ft.
6. Greenland is the greatest in square miles. Victoria Island is the least in square miles.

**Bonus Box Answer:** Answers will vary.

## Page 17
Possible student drawings:

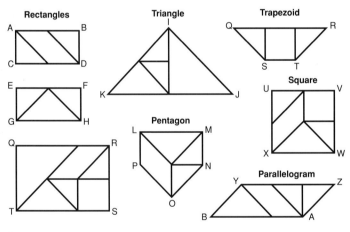

## Page 21
1. obtuse
2. acute
3. right
4. obtuse
5. acute
6. obtuse
7. Drive west on Croaker Lane. Then turn north onto Carp Avenue. Finally, turn east onto Pike Street.
8. Drive east on Bass Street and turn northwest onto Carp Avenue. Then turn east onto Croaker Lane. Next turn northwest onto Bluegill Avenue. Finally, turn east onto Pike Street.

**Bonus Box Answer:** one acute-angled turn, two obtuse-angled turns, and two right-angled turns

## Page 25

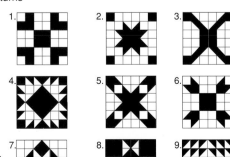

**Bonus Box Answer:** Students' designs will vary.

## Page 29
1. 12, P; Multiples of two are alternated with multiples of three.
2. 22, H; Every other number is half of the number two positions before it.
3. N, E; The number of positions between each letter increases by one: (one letter space—A), B, (two letter spaces—C, D), E, (three letter spaces—F, G, H), I, (four letter spaces—J, K, L, M), N, (five letter spaces—O, P, Q, R, S), T.
4. 1000001, C; One zero is removed from the middle of each successive number.
5. V, R; The number of positions skipped between each letter alternates by three positions and then two positions: A, (three letter spaces—B, C, D), E, (two letter spaces—F, G), H, (three letter spaces—I, J, K), L, (two letter spaces—M, N), O, (three letter spaces—P, Q, R), S, (two letter spaces—T, U), V, (three letter spaces—W, X, Y), Z.
6. 16, A; Each successive number is twice the number before it.
7. Y, P; The letters N and Y alternate with repeating patterns—for N: single N, single N, double N; for Y: single Y, double Y.
8. 21, P; Each successive number is subtracted from the one before it.
9. ■, E; The squares and triangles alternate with repeating patterns—for the square: two squares, one square; for the triangle: pointing down, pointing up.
10. ■■, P; The triangles and squares alternate with a repeating pattern—triangles that decrease in number by one, and squares that increase in number by one.
11. 10, T; Every other number is two less than the number two positions before it.

Secret message: The missing peppers are in the *pepper patch!*

## Page 33
Answers may vary.
1. 3 x 4 = 12 *or* 4 x 3 = 12 *or* 3 + 3 + 3 + 3 = 12
2. 1 + 3 + 1 + 3 + 1 = 9
3. 3 + 2 + 3 + 2 + 2 = 15
4. 7 x 2 = 14 *or* 2 x 7 = 14 *or* 2 + 2 + 2 + 2 + 2 + 2 + 2 = 14
5. 6 x 1 = 6 *or* 1 x 6 = 6 *or* 1 + 1 + 1 + 1 + 1 + 1 = 6
6. 6 x 3 = 18 *or* 3 x 6 = 18 *or* 3 + 3 + 3 + 3 + 3 + 3 = 18
7. Answers will vary.

**Bonus Box Answer:** Answers will vary.

## Page 37
1. 20 cm
2. 27 cm
3. 16 cm
4. 23 cm
5. 24 cm
6. 16 cm
7. 26 cm
8. 46 cm
9. Oliver; Fiona and Kathleen
10. Donna—$30.00; Oliver—$40.50; Fiona—$24.00; Ryan—$34.50; Jamie—$36.00; Kathleen—$24.00; Zack—$39.00

**Bonus Box Answer:** $148.50

## Page 41
1. l = 4 cm; w = 3 cm
   Area = 12 square cm
2. l = 3 cm; w = 2 cm
   Area = 6 square cm
3. l = 4 cm; w = 2 cm
   Area = 8 square cm
4. l = 5 cm; w = 3 cm
   Area = 15 square cm
5. l = 3 cm; w = 3 cm
   Area = 9 square cm
6. l = 6 cm; w = 2 cm
   Area = 12 square cm
7. l = 5 cm; w = 2 cm
   Area = 10 square cm
8. l = 6 cm; w = 3 cm
   Area = 18 square cm
9. Section 8; Section 2
10. 90 aphids

**Bonus Box Answer:** 8 square cm greater

## Page 45
1. 2 hours 9 minutes
2. 1 hour 33 minutes
3. 3 hours 15 minutes
4. 1 hour 57 minutes
5. 3 hours
6. 1 hour 17 minutes
7. 1 hour 10 minutes
8. 2 hours 22 minutes
9. 45 minutes
10. 3 hours 50 minutes
11. 1 hour 27 minutes
12. 35 minutes
13. 3 hours 6 minutes
14. 8 hours 17 minutes

**Bonus Box Answer:** 11 hours: 1 hour 33 minutes + 1 hour 10 minutes + 8 hours 17 minutes

# Page 49

| Day | 1 | 2 | 3 | 4 | 5 | 6 | 7 | 8 | 9 | 10 | 11 | 12 | 13 | 14 | 15 | 16 | 17 | 18 | 19 | 20 | 21 |
|---|---|---|---|---|---|---|---|---|---|---|---|---|---|---|---|---|---|---|---|---|---|
| Monkeys | | X | | | X | | | X | | | | X | | | X | | | X | | | X |
| Elephants | | | | X | | | | | | | | X | | | | | | X | | | |

Shana will feed the monkeys and elephants on the same day
three times during a three-week period.

| Day | 1 | 2 | 3 | 4 | 5 | 6 | 7 | 8 | 9 | 10 | 11 | 12 | 13 | 14 |
|---|---|---|---|---|---|---|---|---|---|---|---|---|---|---|
| Josh | | X | | X | | X | | X | | X | | X | | X |
| CJ | | | X | | | X | | | X | | | X | | |

Josh and CJ will work together twice in the next two weeks.

| Customer | 1 | 2 | 3 | 4 | 5 | 6 | 7 | 8 | 9 | 10 | 11 | 12 | 13 | 14 | 15 |
|---|---|---|---|---|---|---|---|---|---|---|---|---|---|---|---|
| Drink | | X | | | X | | | X | | | | X | | | X |
| Pizza | | | X | | | X | | | X | | | X | | | |
| Ice Cream | | | | | | X | | | | | | X | | | |

| Customer | 16 | 17 | 18 | 19 | 20 | 21 | 22 | 23 | 24 | 25 | 26 | 27 | 28 | 29 | 30 |
|---|---|---|---|---|---|---|---|---|---|---|---|---|---|---|---|
| Drink | | | X | | | | X | | | X | | | | | |
| Pizza | X | | | X | | | | | X | | | X | | | |
| Ice Cream | | X | | | | | | | X | | | | | | X |

Three customers bought ice cream and a drink. Two customers
bought all three items.

**Bonus Box Answer:** Josh and CJ will work together seven times
during the next six weeks.

# Page 53

Suggested answers: *(Other answers are possible.)*
1. nachos, chili dog, corn dog, and two soft drinks
2. soft drink, nachos, candy bar, iced tea, and popcorn
3. gum and peanuts
4. hot chocolate and peanuts
5. hot chocolate, two soft drinks, corn dog, cotton candy, and peanuts
6. iced tea, soft drink, cotton candy, candy bar, and ice cream
7. 7, 6, 2, 1
8. 4, 1, 2, 3
9. 7, 6, 5, 7
10. 2, 3, 5, 7
11. 5, 4, 7, 5
12. 6, 7, 4, 1

**Bonus Box Answer:** Students' answers will vary.

# Page 57

| | mowing grass | baby-sitting | grooming pets | washing cars |
|---|---|---|---|---|
| Carrie | ✗ | ✗ | ✓ | ✗ |
| Andrew | ✓ | ✗ | ✗ | ✗ |
| Jake | ✗ | ✓ | ✗ | ✗ |
| Jennifer | ✗ | ✗ | ✗ | ✓ |

| | Halfback Hostel | Goalie Getaway | Sweeper Suite | Defender's Den |
|---|---|---|---|---|
| Carrie | ✗ | ✓ | ✗ | ✗ |
| Andrew | ✗ | ✗ | ✓ | ✗ |
| Jake | ✓ | ✗ | ✗ | ✗ |
| Jennifer | ✗ | ✗ | ✗ | ✓ |

**Bonus Box Answer:** Students' problems will vary.

# Page 65
1. 6 combinations: TC, TP, HC, HP, CD/C, CD/P
2. 12 combinations: TM, TJ, TS, PM, PJ, PS, HM, HJ, HS, BM, BJ, BS
3. 18 combinations: TCM, TCJ, TCS, TPM, TPJ, TPS, HCM, HCJ,
   HCS, HPM, HPJ, HPS, CD/CM, CD/CJ, CD/CS, CD/PM, CD/PJ,
   CD/ PS
4. 7 combinations: S, C, V, SC, SV, CV, SCV
5. 7 more choices: SF, CF, VF, SCF, SVF, CVF, SCVF

## Page 77
1. 1/6
2. 1/8
3. 3/5
4. 1/2
5. 3/6 or 1/2
6. 1/2
7. 2/10 or 1/5
8. 4/11
9. 7/15
10. 3/8

# Page 85
1. 5/12 + 2/12 = 7/12; U
2. 13/14 – 3/14 = 10/14 = 5/7; T
3. 7/15 + 3/15 = 10/15 = 2/3; F
4. 13/16 – 9/16 = 4/16 = 1/4; A
5. 4/10 + 1/10 = 5/10 = 1/2; !
6. 8/9 – 1/9 = 7/9; A
7. 3/18 + 7/18 = 10/18 = 5/9; E
8. 1/6 + 1/6 = 2/6 = 1/3; T
9. 20/21 – 17/21 = 3/21 = 1/7; O
10. 9/16 + 5/16 = 14/16 = 7/8; T
11. 5/15 – 2/15 = 3/15 = 1/5; O
12. 7/16 – 5/16 = 2/16 = 1/8; C
13. 2/7 + 5/7 = 7/7 = 1; T
14. 11/12 – 1/12 = 10/12 = 5/6; G
15. 7/10 + 1/10 = 8/10 = 4/5; I
16. 9/11 – 2/11 = 7/11; H
17. 1/9 + 3/9 = 4/9; S
18. 17/25 – 7/25 = 10/25 = 2/5; B
19. 1/8 + 5/8 = 6/8 = 3/4; H
20. 19/20 – 1/20 = 18/20 = 9/10; E

Answer to riddle: *The cat is out of the bag!*

# Page 89
1. 56 days
2. 24
3. 48 inches
4. $0.96
5. 6, 12, 18
6. 28
7. 5
8. 18 angles
9. 45 square units
10. 22.5
11. 1,000
12. 4 1/2 hours
13. 82
14. 20 sides
15. $0.68
16. 180 minutes
17. $7.55
18. 45,900
19. 8, 16, 24, 32
20. 25
21. 14 units
22. $1.09
23. 92 days
24. 16
25. 3 1/2 hours

# Page 93

| | M | T | W | Th | F | Weekly Total | Average |
|---|---|---|---|---|---|---|---|
| Nicholas | 5 | 7 | 5 | 5 | 8 | 30 | 6 |
| Angela | 9 | 8 | 4 | 6 | 3 | 30 | 6 |
| Alexander | 6 | 4 | 8 | 5 | 2 | 25 | 5 |
| Gregory | 7 | 5 | 10 | 4 | 4 | 30 | 6 |
| Sarah | 10 | 4 | 6 | 7 | 3 | 30 | 6 |
| Jackie | 5 | 8 | 9 | 9 | 4 | 35 | 7 |
| **Daily Total** | 42 | 36 | 42 | 36 | 24 | 180 | 36 |
| **Average** | 7 | 6 | 7 | 6 | 4 | 30 | |

1. Jackie
2. Monday
3. higher
4. Friday

**Bonus Box Answer:** Answers will
vary depending on student problems.

# Page 61
1. There are 36 stamps on the border of a 10 x 10 sheet of 100
   stamps.
2. Farmer Ted has five goats and four chickens.
3. Mrs. Foster's class needs to walk four blocks north.
4. It will take 15 races to declare a winner.

5 goats            4 chickens

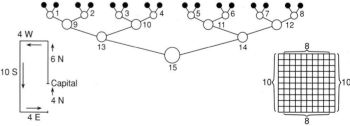

**Bonus Box Answer:** Farmer Ted has six goats and seven chickens.

# Page 69
1. Tia had $49.00 before she bought the hat and sweatshirt.
2. Jacob's mom bought a bag of candy that contained 76 pieces.
3. Trina had $100.00 in her piggy bank.
4. Antawn started his baseball-card collection with 25 cards.
5. Gabriella spent $30.73 on CDs.
6. Dominick's school had 60 students enrolled during its first year.